POWERS

TESTING THE PSYCHIC & SUPERNATURAL

Dan Korem

INTERVARSITY PRESS
DOWNERS GROVE, ILLINOIS 60515

InterVarsity Press is the book-publishing division of InterVarsity Christian Fellowship, a student movement active on campus at hundreds of universities, colleges and schools of nursing. For information about local and regional activities, write Public Relations Dept., InterVarsity Christian Fellowship, 6400 Schroeder Rd., P.O. Box 7895, Madison, WI 53707-7895.

Distributed in Canada through InterVarsity Press, 860 Denison St., Unit 3, Markham, Ontario L3R 4H1, Canada.

Scripture quotations, unless otherwise noted, are from the Holy Bible: New International Version. © 1978 by the New York International Bible Society. Used by permission of Zondervan Bible Publishers.

Cover photograph: Michael Goss

Edited by Dave and Neta Jackson

ISBN 0-8308-1277-6

Printed in the United States of America

Library of Congress Cataloging in Publication Data

Korem, Danny.
    Powers: testing the psychic and supernatural/Dan Korem.
      p.   cm.
    Includes bibliographical references.
    ISBN 0-8308-1277-6
      1. Psychical research—Controversial literature.   2. Christianity
and parapsychology.   3. Impostors and imposture.   4. Hydrick, James.
I. Title.
BF1042.K68 1988
133—dc19   88-13029
                                           CIP

17	16	15	14	13	12	11	10	9	8	7	6	5	4	3	2	1
99	98	97	96	95	94	93	92	91	90	89	88					

Dedicated to my kids,
Carrie, Erik, and Luke,
who test their dad's
powers everyday

Only a Moment

I am a journalist in both the print and electronic media who investigates and reports on exotic types of deception. The broad context of what I investigate relates to societal trends of deception and why we are all vulnerable to having our thought process short-circuited. Psychics, healers and others who claim to have powers have been my particular focus over the last few years. My interest was sparked due to my former profession.

Prior to 1981 I earned my livelihood solely as a professional magician. Since I was a teen, I could perform tricks which people thought were powers. This raised a question in my mind: are there any real powers? And so began an unusual hunt.

There are essentially five lines of thought concerning claims of supernatural and paranormal powers. You, the reader, fall into one of them.

The first group believes in supernatural powers as well as mind powers—powers that don't have anything to do with supernatural forces.

A second group believes in mind powers but doesn't believe in supernatural powers.

A third group believes in the possibility of supernatural powers but not in mind powers.

A fourth group believes in simply an external "force," although this group can't exactly define what it means.

A fifth group doesn't believe in any of these options.

In this book, I have tried to select cases and shed perspective that will aid all five groups in becoming more discerning.

What is covered here is not a pop issue, as it is often treated in the press, but represents the essence of what we believe about our existence. Each case has been thoroughly researched relying on video and audio tape footage, reliable sources whose input has measured up against the test of time or (when in doubt) by corroboration by at least two sources related to a specific case when confirming specific data. Names and places in certain instances have of course been changed to protect privacy.

As per the counsel of my good friend Dr. Ray Hyman, professor of psychology at the University of Oregon, I have included my perspective regarding my own personal faith in the latter section of the text. Although not the norm in an investigative text, he felt it would better give both the believer and nonbeliever a more complete context in which to study the claims of power covered in this text.

I hope my colleagues in the art of legerdemain will not be too disgruntled by the exposure of two or three effects which are seldom used. Their inclusion is to aid those who do not have an understanding of sophisticated trickery, thus enabling them to be less vulnerable when confronted with something which appears to be a power.

Those to whom appreciation is due for assistance on this project are: my wife Sandy, who provides a clear sounding board for all my adventures; Jon Racherbaumer, who forces me to think and rethink about the things which are important; and Jim Sire, Andy Le Peau and Don Stephenson of the editorial staff at InterVarsity Press for insightful input.

Chapter 1

Belief
and Faith
in the Balance

CAREFULLY CHOOSING HER WORDS, THE TELEVISION REPORTER SEATED IN MY Dallas office asked me the same question for the third time: "But can't you believe just by faith? I mean, do you *have* to have proof for everything?"

Her persistence surprised me. Denise wanted to know why I wouldn't believe in psychics and miracles by faith alone. In over ten years of fielding reporters' questions in all kinds of contexts, this was the first time that a reporter actually seemed annoyed by my response.

"Yes. In order for me to believe in something that is supernatural or paranormal, I have to have something tangible that would justify my belief."

Investigating claims of "powers" usually gives rise to the same kinds of questions: "Have you ever found someone who really has powers?" "Do you believe in God?" "Do you believe in demons?" "Are you afraid that someone you expose may come after you?" "How do you explain the fact that I always know when my husband will call?"

Often the motivating factor behind such questions is personal curiosity. Most of us are intrigued by mysteries we don't fully understand. This reporter's question was not unique. But the way Denise asked it was. She was visibly disturbed.

Television and radio reporters tend to use a deeper voice when asking questions to maintain an authoritative air, one that is in command of the facts. Denise's voice, however, began to climb as she inched forward, betraying her exasperation with my unwillingness to yield on this point. It caught me off guard.

A reporter's job is to put together a story as objectively as possible. But in this case I wondered whether the story hit too close to home. Perhaps the subject related to her *personally.*

"I receive calls in my office every week," I continued, "where people claim that someone has been miraculously healed or has predicted the future or some psychic is helping police solve a homicide, just to name a few examples. As a journalist, if I just *believe* one of these reports without verification, I am no longer reporting facts in a context that will help people. I might actually become party to a deception, and I don't want to aid in someone buying into a lie."

"I realize that you have a professional commitment," she responded, "but what about you personally? Can't you just accept something by faith? Do you always have to have proof?" she asked with greater insistence.

"When it comes to claims of power, the answer is the same, even personally," I responded.

It was obvious to me and her camera crew that she was frustrated by my stance, that I was too rigid, too close-minded. I suspected that she had experienced something in her life which she believed to be supernatural or psychic, even though she couldn't prove it. Maybe she was hoping I would assure her that it is okay to "just believe," as she put it.

Later I discovered from a mutual friend that she had indeed had an experience which she was convinced was supernatural. I never found out what her experience was exactly. Had we met in a more informal setting, she might have felt at ease telling me about it.

Investigating a Miracle

For several weeks after the interview with the reporter in my Dallas office, I was disturbed. I knew that my answer was inadequate for her; or better stated, I hadn't fully thought through the question. After some reflection, I realized that she was actually asking two different questions. First, do claims of supernatural or psychic powers have to be verified with hard facts before they can be believed? And second, is it all right to believe in something by faith alone? That is, is it okay to believe in something we can't prove with facts but which we still believe is true?

These kinds of honest questions go right to the heart of who we are and what we believe. The quest for facts and proof appeals to our mind and intellect, while exercising faith is a matter of the heart and spirit— though hopefully after careful thought and consideration.

I wrestled with her question until it finally dawned on me how I should have responded. I should have told her that when I look at a case where there is a report of supposed supernatural or psychic powers, I have to verify that something *did* or *did not* take place. Morally and journalistically it's my responsibility.

For example, let's imagine that a nine-year-old boy, whom we will call Jimmy, was born blind. His eyes are deformed and are half the size of a marble. Jimmy's parents, who attend church faithfully, asked for those in their Sunday-school class to pray that God would heal their son's eyes. They requested this after a friend suggested, "What could it hurt?" The class compassionately agreed.

The next Sunday everyone was jubilant. The class members could

hardly believe it. Jimmy could see. Apparently while Jimmy was saying
his prayers before he went to bed on Friday night, he felt a burning
sensation in his eyes and began crying out. Thinking he might have hurt
himself, his parents ran to his room to find Jimmy sitting on the floor
rubbing his eyes. But Jimmy looked up and, for the first time in his life,
saw the outline of his parents standing in the doorway. In a matter of
hours, he could see both of them in perfect detail. His eyes are now
perfectly formed.

After hearing the teary-eyed parents relate what happened, the class
collectively acknowledged that God had answered their prayers.

Here we have a situation where a boy, blind since birth, can now see.
But before reporting that a *physical* miracle has occurred, we first have
to verify that Jimmy *was* blind.

Presumably this would be easy to confirm because of the medical
reports of various doctors who had examined him. His condition would
have been obvious to any doctor, indeed, anyone looking at the child.
In addition, there is no chance that his condition could have had a
psychological origin.

If the leading ophthalmologist concurred that a spontaneous recovery
is impossible, then we would have irrefutable proof that *something*
extraordinary had happened to Jimmy's eyes.

No faith would be required to believe these *facts*.

When Faith Is Appropriate

There is a part of this story, however, which could never be verified by
facts. You'll remember that Jimmy's parents and the Sunday-school class
believed that *God* healed his eyes. To believe that God was the cause
of the restoration of sight required faith on their part.

As a journalist, I could record with my camera the testimony of the
doctors who examined Jimmy before and after his sight returned. I
could even interview those who prayed for Jimmy's healing. But I would
never be able to make an appointment with God for an interview and
with my camera crew confirm that he actually healed Jimmy.

If I could, I would have all kinds of questions for him like: "How did you heal Jimmy? What kind of power did you use to do that? Why did you heal Jimmy and not the Garabaldi boy down the street from me who has multiple sclerosis? If you can heal people, how come you make some folks smart enough to be doctors so they can treat and heal people? Aren't you running the risk of letting us humans think that we are the solution to life's problems instead of you?"

These and other questions would be relevant to most of us, and we would like to know the answers. But the fact remains that I will not get that interview with God to establish *why* or *how* Jimmy was healed . . . at least not in this life. It requires faith to believe in God. Most of us have never visually seen God or audibly heard him speak; therefore, it requires faith to believe that God healed Jimmy. But it does *not* require faith to believe that Jimmy can now see. So how *does* one tackle a case like what has just been described—like the scores of other cases I receive every year?

It doesn't matter if I am investigating a psychic who claims to predict the future, a psychic who police believe can help solve a homicide or a miracle that someone believes has happened. My job as a journalist who investigates these things is to establish what happened.

Then I try to find the reason *why* it did or did not take place, and *who* is or isn't behind it. As a professional, that's my job. I have to report the facts, even if they contradict what I personally would like to believe.

Blind vs. Informed Faith

Though not trained as a journalist, I have been drawn into investigating psychic and supernatural phenomena from a unique perspective. I started studying the art of sleight of hand when I was nine years old in Wilmette, a suburb of Chicago.

One of the most valuable lessons that I learned early on was that a good magician does *not* rely upon the hand being quicker than the eye. Rather, one must misdirect the spectator's *thoughts* so that they cannot unravel the secret. If I simply make a quick move to accomplish an effect, the audience might be fooled for the moment. But when they get home and have time to think and discuss a particular trick, the secret might be uncovered. So the goal is to set little mental land mines that will explode *any* conceivable theory.

If a spectator thinks that he or she knows the secret—even if the proposed theory is wrong—the illusion is spoiled because in their mind they think they know how it's done. This is true even if the spectator is correct. It is for this reason that I spend an average of two to three years (I have spent up to seven) perfecting a trick to discover every conceivable explanation someone might put forth. Even Houdini, if he were alive today, would be fooled by today's state-of-the-art legerdemain.

By the time I was fifteen, I began to invent and perform mentalism tricks. These are tricks which appear to be mind powers: reading someone's mind, predicting the future or moving an object by apparent mind control. I was amazed that most adults believed that the modus operandi was by psychic abilities. They could not fathom that a teen-ager could fool them. They were wrong. Anyone can be fooled, myself included.

For me this raised an obvious question. Are there real powers? Or are we deceived by misreports, deception and a lack of information? So I began tracking down stories where people believed that they had a psychic or supernatural experience. Simultaneously I corresponded and met with some of the leading magicians in this country to increase my repertoire.

Then, when I was a senior in high school, I stumbled across some members of my family huddled around a Ouija board. They were trying to find out what had happened to a relative with connections to organized crime. He had been missing for several months. The slow-moving planchette, under the fingertips of a highly educated relative, spelled out that he was safe and living in Israel. But a few months later, he was found dead in a shallow grave in Canada. Those with misplaced hope were devastated.

It was then that I determined not to accept anything but the facts.

I began collecting underground books and manuals written for fortune tellers, readers and seers, and incorporated some of their techniques into my presentations. I didn't do this to convince others I had powers, but rather to show how these deceptions can mirror what appears to be a power.

In 1970, as a freshman at Tulane University in New Orleans, Jon Racherbaumer, one of the world's foremost authors of texts for magicians, befriended me. Ten years my senior, he challenged me to innovate my own material. Together we later published a number of texts.

More important than his introducing me to the undefined "inner circle" of magicians and their secrets were our discussions concerning the mental process of deception. We observed that the same psychological principles that we used to fool an audience were the same principles which short-circuited our judgment in everyday life. This observation helped me to understand not just how the uninitiated are fooled, but more importantly *why* people were deceived by power fakers.

While a student, I was frequently invited to be the guest on local radio talk shows when psychics, spiritists and others were to appear. New Orleans, with its culture rich in voodoo and the occultic arts, was a natural stopping-off point for those selling their wares. I appeared with these esoteric guests not as a skeptic, but rather one who knew about deception and was honestly curious.

Never knowing what to expect, I became increasingly disappointed to discover that none had any powers. Most were outright charlatans and at best simply self-deceived. Not surprisingly, a belief in God was usually interwoven in their pitch to appeal to a broader constituency.

Whenever God was mentioned as the source of their power, I listened attentively. Only a year before, I embraced the Christian faith, having been reared in the Jewish faith. I still considered myself Jewish, but a Jew who believed that Jesus, the Nazarene, was the long-promised Messiah. At times it was confusing when I would talk to God-fearing people who were duped by the psychic crowd. Were the powers real? And were they of human or supernatural origin? The rationale that was often inferred was that God can do anything, so one shouldn't question. To question was to lack faith. For me faith wasn't the problem. It was the unfounded claims of power that I witnessed.

I believed that there was a God with unlimited powers, but at the same time I knew, because of my training, that friends of mine were honestly mistaken. In retrospect, I can see how these early experiences contributed to the development of a discerning mindset. If I was going to express my faith in something, it would be as a result of a measure of substance and not blind faith.

By blind faith I mean the kind of faith where people choose to believe—for no rhyme or reason—exactly what they want to believe, even if the facts lead to another conclusion. An example of blind faith was my dialog with a woman who believed that her daily horoscope could predict her future. Even after I explained that study after study has demonstrated that the horoscope cannot predict the future, she said, "Well, that's just what I want to believe." This is the essence of blind faith. It is faith where the use of one's mind is put on the shelf, and facts and information are considered irrelevant.

I personally have yet to meet or hear of someone who actually has psychic powers. By psychic powers I am referring to something the *brain* can do *in and of its own ability,* like reading someone else's mind or moving objects without touching them.

It's important to understand that when we talk about *psychic* powers, we're talking about *human* powers and not *supernatural* powers. You see, when I began investigating the possibility of *human* psychic abilities, I didn't have any preconceived ideas one way or the other. I simply didn't know if such a thing existed.

Scientists, however, who have spent millions of dollars over the last fifty years to find real human psychic powers, have come up empty-handed. They have yet to find even one case of real psychic powers (also referred to as ESP—extrasensory perception).

Because of the lack of evidential proof, plus my own experience in tracking down hundreds of alleged cases of psychic powers over the last fifteen years without finding one to be bona fide, I have decided not to put my *faith* in the belief that human psychic powers exist. There just isn't any evidence to support that notion. If any credible evidence is ever brought forward, I will gladly change my position.

Substantive Faith

Faith based upon a measure of substance is another matter. According to Hebrews 11:1, "Faith is being sure of what we hope for and certain of what we do not see." Let's look at this succinct definition of faith in the light of investigating the claims of psychic and supernatural powers.

When exercising faith, we must clearly define *what* it is that we believe in. In other words, what is it that we *hope* is true? If I say that I have faith that human psychic powers will one day be discovered, I must clarify what I mean by psychic powers. What is it that I would expect these powers to do? For example, I could state that I have faith that one day science will discover that my brain emits some kind of energy which can make something move without touching it—*telekinesis.* I would be laying on the line what I explicitly expect to happen. This is the first part of the definition—that is, faith is what I *hope* will be true.

In the second part of the definition in Hebrews, we must be "certain of what we do not see." In other words, there must be a *reason* to believe in something we cannot see.

Imagine scientists conducting an experiment where a person, seated at a table, intensely concentrates on a three-pound steel ball. The goal is to try and make the ball move without touching it. After several minutes it is detected both by sensors and cameras that the ball starts to move—it actually moves. Trickery, vibrations and other assorted explanations are then ruled out by qualified experts. In addition, the sensors monitoring the subject's brain detected no unusual brain activity. Although the ball moved, we don't know how.

Now at this point we may express our *faith* that the subject's brain caused the movement, even though we haven't yet detected how the brain did it. Why? Because the ball moved.

In this example we have defined what we *hope* will be discovered—that the brain possesses telekinetic powers—and we are *certain* of what we can't see because the steel ball moved. A paranormal event has been verified, and a person could now choose to believe that one day the human power will be identified.

I have chosen, however, *not* to put my faith in that hope precisely because this example is entirely imaginary. There are no verifiable telekinetic phenomena on record.

At the same time, I wouldn't choose to exercise my faith and believe in the resurrection of Christ—an alleged supernatural event that is the heart of Christianity—unless there was a measure of substantive proof like reliable historical records of the time. Even Christ himself said, "Believe me when I say that I am in the Father and the Father is in me; or at least believe on the evidence of the miracles themselves" (Jn 14:11). In a later chapter we'll look at some interesting evidence surrounding his life, death and resurrection.

But for now, let's start with an underlying premise: When it comes to claims of power, we must first find out if the claim is valid. Then you or I can offer our opinion as to what *caused* it to happen.

Visually Present the Facts

Prior to producing my first television special, *Psychic Confessions,* the exposé of a man alleged to be the world's leading psychic, I became convinced that just giving people the facts is usually insufficient to change their beliefs if they have been taken in. It helps greatly if the proof is visual and incontrovertible. Great sensitivity must be exercised toward the person taken in because one is touching raw exposed nerves of belief.

That is why I have opted to be an *electronic* investigative journalist—someone who reports via a visual medium like television, although I also do some work in the print media. For the type of cases I investigate, nothing is more powerful than actual videotaped footage to report the facts and the impact of fraud on the human psyche.

There is an expression that "the eye of a camera never blinks." Obviously this is slightly overstated since a cameraman might have his power cut off, a field producer can request a certain angle for a shot which might be misleading or an editor can cut the real story out of a piece. But generally speaking, the raw uncut footage doesn't lie. If an ethical journalist takes raw footage and selects the best segments, the real story is easier to believe as the truth. To this end, video pictures are almost always better for verifying claims of power than still photographs, listening to the spoken word or reading a printed account.

In one case, I filmed a woman who had appeared on several national radio talk shows. She was supposed to be able to predict the future with her psychic powers. As I interviewed her I realized that the talk show hosts had been exploiting her (and their audiences) in a rather cruel way. Not only could she not predict the future, but on video it was obvious that she was in need of psychiatric care. Out of sensitivity to the woman, I decided not to air the footage of my interview.

Claims of power affect the very essence of what we believe and in turn affect our view of the world and how we live our lives on our hurried planet. The search and attainment of paranormal powers is heady stuff. Many seek to get a grip on and control the uncontrollable through the promise of personal power—psychic and supernatural powers.

The reporter who initially asked me, "But can't you just believe by faith?" really wanted to know if what she had experienced was supernatural. Even with her training as a reporter, she didn't know how to record and validate what she believed she had experienced.

What is the real story? Is there something out there—psychic or supernatural—that is real?

To find out, let's begin with a look at those who claim to be able to read minds, tell the future and reveal intimate details about the lives of people they have just met. Let's meet the "cold reading" psychic.

Part I
Cold Readings

Chapter 2

Beating Three Psychics at Their Own Game

ALMOST EVERY WEEK I RECEIVE A CALL FROM OR ON BEHALF OF A VICTIM OF someone who claims to have powers. In the last year the cases have included a homicide and felonies where large sums of money are involved. At the other end of the spectrum are your garden-variety psychics or gypsies who advertise in the local TV Times and are out to make a fast buck—at someone else's expense. I have even received calls from business executives who have had psychics convince them to keep them on retainer for sums of up to $1,500 per month.

Age, education, status in the community, and intelligence are not factors when it comes to being taken in. Most formal and informal polls conducted over the last ten years indicate that a majority of the population have had what they believe to be a psychic or supernatural experience. This sets up a societal environment that gives instant credibility to a psychic.

The Attraction

Many people are often drawn to consult a psychic by nothing more than what one talk-show host described as "just fun and games," some high-spirited excitement in a mystical atmosphere. Others visit these modern day "wise men and women" out of curiosity, often sparked by a friend who was impressed on a previous visit. And then there are those who are desperate and seek help with a problem in their personal lives. They have unsuccessfully sought help elsewhere, and the psychic is their last resort.

But for whatever reason, this seemingly harmless activity can serve as an intriguing entry-level activity into more harmful practices.

In 1986 an executive with a large corporation asked me to help him gather evidence related to the murder of his seventeen-year-old son, Jim. It was an unusual case that had local authorities stymied. It revolved around pseudo-occultic activities where there were no real powers operative, but where Jim tried to tap into supernatural powers.

(The use of the word *occult* can too often create the mistaken impression that something supernatural is taking place. For example, witches casting spells is occultic, but that doesn't necessarily mean that supernatural occurrences will accompany the spells. For this reason, I choose to use the word *pseudo-occult* to clarify that there are no supernatural powers involved. The game Dungeons and Dragons [D & D] can also be considered pseudo-occultic, but not necessarily supernatural.)

When Jim was ten years old, he started playing D & D. It is an easy-to-purchase game where youngsters create their own mythical characters that they themselves act out. This sounds harmless except that in D & D the players act out the roles of assassins and evil characters who maim and kill people in a bizarre and twisted fashion. Network news reports have covered a number of stories where kids have murdered others or have committed suicide after intense sessions. One CBS report stated that over twenty-five kids have died in cases where it was suspected that D & D was the catalyst that fed young, impressionable minds.

Jim wanted to develop his own powers. When D & D didn't satisfy him, his mother took him to see a psychic who did readings for him, but Jim could never develop the same skills as the psychic. A couple of years later, when Jim was a junior in high school with good grades in an upper-middle-class neighborhood, he hooked up with a man in his twenties who taught him Satanic rituals in exchange for sexual favors. Shortly after he wanted out, he was murdered. The road that eventually led to his death began with a simple game and some sessions with a psychic.

Well, you might reason, of course this could happen to a non-streetwise teen-ager. Now consider the following case that involved a sophisticated professional who wasn't seeking those peddling powers.

A broker for a large stock brokerage firm was in the lobby of the Marriott Hotel in Dallas waiting to meet a business associate for lunch. Arriving several minutes early, the broker took a short stroll around the hotel to kill time and noticed a sign that said "Psychic Fair" posted over one of the large meeting rooms. In passing, the broker asked a well-dressed woman standing in the hallway what it was all about. The woman explained that the Dallas-area psychics were having a fair so people could meet and become acquainted with them and their gifts and abilities. Over fifty psychics were in the room, all at their own tables. And over two hundred people were picking up literature and making appointments. Others were engaged in readings.

Psychic fairs are common in most metropolitan cities, being held several times a year. They sometimes attract thousands. I'm using the term *psychic* (when applied to an individual) for anyone today who claims to predict the future, recall one's past or the like by reading palms, tarot cards (occult cards) or by analyzing a person's aura—an imaginary energy field supposedly likened to Christ's halo. Still others deal in healing crystals that will cure and heal the sick, while some use color analysis to "solve" your problems by better understanding the color of the clothes you wear. Those who are the most talented don't use anything at all. You just sit down and they tell you detailed information about yourself and give advice about how to solve your problems.

Some of this may sound farfetched, but millions of people are hooked on psychic practices. The broker was one who wasn't, however, and he registered skepticism while listening to the woman's short verbal tour. The woman then said, "I know you don't believe in this sort of thing, but would you mind if I do a reading for you right here because I know there is a lot of stress in your life right now."

"Go ahead, I only have a couple of minutes," was the halfhearted, skeptical response.

The Gypsy's Mark
What the broker didn't know was that the woman was a gypsy fortune-teller in a sophisticated guise (sans a dangling earring). She was siphoning off business from the psychics who had rented the room. She then proceeded to identify specific problems in the broker's life, as well as the name of a friend that the broker later said, "She couldn't have known."

He was astounded, and the reader succeeded in scheduling another appointment with him. This led to a series of appointments; each time the gypsy (who called herself a psychic) accurately tuned in to more and more specific information that baffled the broker while she offered advice to solve personal and business problems. In this Faustian relationship the broker became dependent on the reader's advice before making any decisions. Eventually this converted into a fear of missing a visit with her.

Ultimately he agreed to go through a bizarre ritual where crushed eggs were smeared over his body to drive out a "demon spirit." After the ritual, a jar of a viscous fluid was put on the table. A red looking creature was seen floating in the jar. It was the "demon," now exorcised, explained the gypsy.

Several weeks later, I was called to help untangle the web of confusion. First, I explained to him how the reader created the illusion that she knew specific names, dates and so forth. Then I recommended psychiatric counseling to help undo the cerebral manipulation the reader used to develop a dependency on her.

It should be pointed out again that this was the broker's first experience with a psychic. How, you may ask, could a levelheaded person with a healthy degree of skepticism get caught up in something this bizarre? The answer is that the broker didn't have an explanation for the concise revelation of information.

Discernment, Not Skepticism

Skepticism isn't needed so much to combat these claims as discernment. Skepticism is simply a doubting state of mind. A person looks with narrowed eyes and says, "Prove it to me. I'm hard to fool." A discerning person works from a framework that says, "Give me the facts, let me weigh them and then I'll make a decision."

If a shrewd and clever psychic can remove even a portion of a skeptical person's doubts through ruseful maneuvering, then there is a good chance of converting the skeptic. This was the case with the broker. The broker was skeptical and didn't believe someone could actually read thoughts and recall past events. When "proof" was offered, the broker bit because, "I'm naturally skeptical and hard to fool."

My good friend Dr. Ray Hyman, professor of psychology at the University of Oregon and a respected expert on psychological deception, calls this the "illusion of invulnerability"—the "not me" syndrome. The other guy can be fooled but not me. However, studies show that people who don't think they can be deceived are often the easiest to deceive because they are relying on their "skeptical nature" to protect them.

The fact of the matter is that we are all vulnerable and can be deceived. That's why a discerning person who weighs all the possibilities and recognizes that he or she *still* might not know the answer is far less vulnerable than a person who is merely doubting or skeptical.

If the broker had been armed with the little knowledge available in this book, it would probably have been enough to prevent his falling into the psychic's trap. Even if the broker didn't know the specific *techniques* used by the reader, a shorthand knowledge of the available *principles* would have raised enough questions and red flags to short-circuit the reader's deception.

But before examining the actual principles and techniques of the typical reader, let's look at what happened when I went on a television with three psychics.

Three Psychics
In the fall of 1986, I was asked to appear on a popular Detroit talk show with three psychics to represent the other side of the coin.[1] I agreed with the request that I be planted in the audience. I wanted the psychics to do a reading on me *after* they had done readings on other members of the studio audience. The reason was to establish irrefutable proof of how they got their information.

When you simply tell someone how a psychic extracts information, the credibility factor is not nearly as effective as catching the psychic in the act. Then there is no disputing how the psychic gets the information. Otherwise, one must deal with numerous loophole counter-explanations like: "Yes, but I didn't even know I would be at the location where I met the psychic," or "But I tell you, no one knew except me."

Therefore, before the talk show began, I gave the host a letter that stated what the psychics would tell me about myself—with one catch. Everything I stated in the letter was *false*. I did this for demonstration purposes. You see, if I really know *how* readers operate, then I should be able to miscue them with false information. On the other hand, if they were truly psychic, they would circumvent my false information and come up with the real facts.

Dropping the Clues
The three psychics ranged in age from their mid-forties to early fifties.

They were the type of readers usually hired for society parties and fund-raising functions as a part of the entertainment. The talk show host roamed the studio audience with his hand-held microphone, picking people at random for the readings to insure that the psychics had no plants. The psychics—not the best I have seen—hit on enough specifics to elicit gasps from those watching.

Attired in a dress shirt and tie, loosened to convey a relaxed appearance, I was the last one that was asked to stand. With my shoulders slightly stooped and my hands held loosely together in front of me exposing a bare left-hand ring finger, I told the psychics my first name and the reading began. The white skin one normally sees on a finger when the wedding band is removed was covered with make-up. The reason I gave my name is that one of the psychics said that she did her readings solely from hearing a person's name. Of course if the gift were really incarnate in her, she would have known who I really was.

The name-divining psychic started: "You are working on developing your self-confidence, aren't you?"

"Yes," I meekly responded with slumped shoulders.

Then the psychic who read cards said, "You will probably marry a short, dark-haired, mild-mannered girl and she will be good for you. She'll also be a good cook."

I slightly widened my eyes as if she hit a responsive chord. Then I said, "Tell me about Jimmi." As were other members of the audience, I was allowed to ask the psychics about someone I knew.

The third psychic, who worked without props or names, said: "Your business relationship with this man is on shaky ground. You should reevaluate how you work with him. . . . I can't tell if it's in your office or a new business you are considering, but I would just be careful because of his strong feelings and his ability to outmaneuver you, although he may not do this intentionally."

With a flair for the dramatic, the host announced, "This man isn't who you think he is. This is Dan Korem, an investigative journalist and world-class magician! In my coat pocket is a letter that he gave me before the show. Let me read it to you.

"Dear John,

I believe the psychics will tell me the followings things during their reading:

1. I need to work on my confidence with the women that I date.

2. I should be more aggressive in my work.

3. I had a domineering mother or I did not have a positive male role model to whom I could relate in my past.

But unfortunately all of these things do not apply to me. You see, they are false. What these ladies were using is what is called 'cold reading' which I will explain in a few minutes.

By the way, I have been happily married for thirteen years, have three children, and Jimmi is my mother-in-law!

Discerningly yours,

Dan Korem"

The audience reaction was a mix of laughter and amazement. As we went to a commercial break the host said, "When we come back, Dan Korem will explain for us what is known as 'cold reading.' " The response of the psychics was one of nervous fixed composure and forced smiles.

Guys and Grades

After the break, the host asked me, "What is cold reading?" Now seated next to the psychics, I then explained the six points of a successful cold reading, that is, how a psychic can tell a person detailed information without previous contact. Then I pointed to one of the members of the audience, who earlier had been "read," and I asked her to stand. Class was now in session.

"Ma'am, you asked about your daughter who is in college. Correct?" I reconfirmed. The overweight mother in the modest print dress nodded.

"Now, let me ask you something," I said directing my remarks to the whole audience. "What are the two most likely problems a mother who is concerned about her daughter might be willing to share on television? She's not going to talk about a drug or pregnancy problem on live television. So logically, what's left?" I paused, letting everyone consider the options.

"Here's a hint. They both begin with the letter *g*," I led.

"Guys and grades," was the spontaneous response from the audience, as they uncovered the first piece of the puzzle.

"Now the first psychic said, 'Your daughter isn't detail oriented, *is she?*' " I reminded everyone, inflecting the last two words. "Do you remember how she went up on the pitch of her voice when she said, 'is she?'

"Why did she ask that question in that way?" I asked rhetorically. "Well, I'll tell you. See this personality wheel that I am holding? It shows the four basic temperaments and their inherent strengths and weaknesses." (The personality wheel I displayed is on page 34.) Many similar charts have been developed by psychiatrists and psychologists to categorize the various personality traits we all have. I like this particular layout because it's very practical for the lay person to use.

Personality Types

"Now if you study this wheel," I continued, "you will find that a detail-oriented person and a socially-oriented person are opposite personality types on the wheel." I paused to let this sink in. "This is our first clue to how she answered your unspoken question about your daughter," I said, reassuring the attentive mother.

"When she asked you, 'Your daughter isn't detail oriented, is she?,' lilting her voice at the end of her question, you said, 'That's right.' "

The mother, recalling this, nodded.

"Now, if she's not detail oriented, she's likely to be socially oriented, and a student who is socially oriented is likely to be tempted to date too much and let the grades slide. Right?" Everyone nodded in agreement.

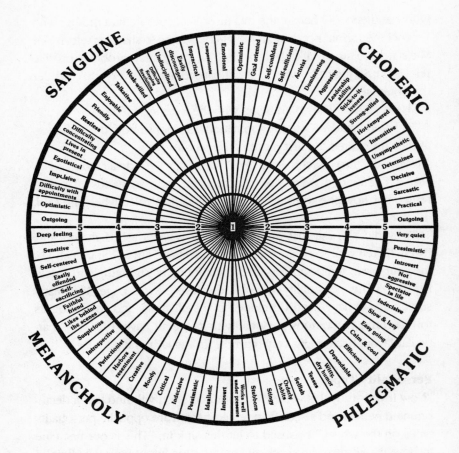

"So it would be a high-percentage guess to say something similar to what the first psychic said, which was: 'Now, if your daughter will pull back on her dating and spend some more time in the books, those grades you are worrying about will come right up. And I know it cost you a lot with that extra job you are carrying to put her through school.' " I could see the lights coming on in the eyes around me.

"The final touch was the psychic's sympathy for you, a working mother trying to get her daughter through school," I said looking at the mother.

"This gives the unspoken appearance that the psychic also knew about your needs by acknowledging that you are working, even though you never told her." She nodded again, starting to catch on.

"How did she know this? She didn't, but for the average family it's necessary that both parents work to help their kids through college; and your modest, but neat dress gave her the needed information that you probably weren't wealthy enough to avoid that task," I said, maintaining reassuring eye contact with the mother. Only a few minutes before she had been really amazed by the psychic's "gift." I wanted to gently let her down in a way that she would know that I cared about her as she came to a clear understanding of what had happened. I didn't want her to feel like an exposed buffoon because she wasn't. She was merely vulnerable, now on her way to discernment.

But What If . . .

"But what if you had said, 'Yes, she is,' when she asked if your daughter is detail oriented?" Again I paused to let everyone sift the question.

"Do you remember how the psychic lilted her voice at the end of the question?" I reminded them. "Your daughter isn't detail oriented, is she?" I repeated, sliding my voice upward.

"That voice inflection was her out. If you had said, 'Yes,' the psychic would have said, 'That's right, and because she is detail oriented, your daughter is probably spending too much time in the books. If she'll lighten up a little, her dating life will get better and I doubt that her grades will suffer.' "

On this last line the whole audience burst out laughing. They realized that they had been had and found the situation humorous while only a few minutes before they had sat stunned and amazed. When people first grasp what is going on, the reaction is usually mixed with laughter. It's like when a person buys a magic trick and reads the instructions. The immediate reaction is, "So that's how it's done! I can't believe it's that simple."

I was never derogatory toward the three psychics. I figure if the goods are put on the table, it's up to the audience to decide. My chastising the psychics in that forum would have been counterproductive. I wanted the audience to weigh the facts, not the personalities involved. I have found that once confronted with the facts honestly delivered with compassion, most folks respond accordingly.

There is a funny ending to this episode. During the next commercial break, the third psychic asked me, "Where can I get hold of that chart?" as she peered over my shoulder trying to get a better look.

I turned it face-down so she couldn't see it. Why give her an edge? If anyone is to have an edge it should be you, right? So let's look at the six principles that make for a successful cold reading. Then you and your friends can discern for yourselves the claims of your neighborhood psychic, fortune teller, reader, or whatever they might call themselves.

Chapter 3

The Art of Cold Reading

THERE ARE SIX PRINCIPLES ONE MUST MASTER TO BECOME AN EXPERT COLD reader. Most psychics are self-taught and learn by trial and error, and a few are even unconscious of the techniques they use, believing the resulting insights are actually psychic or supernatural. However, others can specifically articulate how to effectively cold read. I have a number of underground publications which detail their methods. Here is a short excerpt from one manual.

This is a book about "reading"—primarily "cold" readings.

In a way, I am somewhat sorry that this publication is being released as, over the many years that I have performed, read and counseled, I have always been rather jealous of the knowledge that I have accumulated and have felt that the best way to learn this trade was by hard experience. . . .

There will be occasions, particularly in private readings, when the client's errors or the unsolvable problem must be faced. Such unfortunate instances will require all the skill, ingenuity, counseling psychology and positive support the reader can muster.[1]

Many psychics, like the one above, fancy themselves as legitimate counselors. However, the premise for their counseling is couched in deception since the psychic never tells the client cold reading is being used to gain information and give guidance.

The purpose of describing the six principles for cold reading and how they can be applied is not so that you can become a reader, but rather to enable you to be able to recognize when the principles are being used. Then you or someone you know won't buy into the reader's wares.

While the principles don't change, the applications of these principles (the techniques) will vary with each reader and the surrounding circumstances. The techniques are usually invented on the fly; the rule of thumb is to use whatever works without getting caught.

As you read through each principle and the accompanying examples, keep in mind that a good reader will use more than one principle at a time so their use is never apparent.

1. The Barnum Effect

Most readers usually start with general comments that can relate to anyone. This is called the Barnum Effect. Here is an example:

Some of your aspirations tend to be pretty unrealistic.

At times you are extroverted, affable, sociable, while at other times you are introverted, wary, and reserved. You have found it unwise to be too frank in revealing yourself to others. You pride yourself on being an independent thinker and do not accept others' opinions without satisfactory proof. You prefer a certain amount of change and variety, and become dissatisfied when hemmed in by restrictions and limitations. At times you have serious doubts as to whether you have made the right decision or done the right thing. Disciplined and controlled on the outside, you tend to be worrisome and insecure on the inside. Your sexual adjustment has presented some problems for you. While you have some personality weaknesses, you are generally able to compensate for them. You have a great deal of unused capacity which you have not turned to your advantage. You have a tendency to be critical of yourself. You have a strong need for other people to like you and for them to admire you.[2]

In actual use, the "stock" spiel is delivered in a conversational tone that matches the reader's and client's personalities as well as the tenor of the environment. It may be delivered forcefully, laid back, slightly aloof—in other words, whatever suits the occasion. With some refinement the stock reading can be tailored for a particular individual. Here is one developed for a college student.

You are a person who is very normal in his attitudes, behavior and relationships with people. You get along well without effort. People naturally like you and you are not overly critical of them or yourself. You are neither overly conventional nor overly individualistic. Your prevailing mood is one of optimism and constructive effort, and you are not troubled by periods of depression, psychosomatic illnesses or nervous symptoms.[3]

In this example, an adept reader reassures the student that he is "okay" even though he is going through "changes." If one were doing a reading for a student radical, this stock opening would have to take on a more cause-oriented appeal, rather then a blending effect.

I recently had lunch with the head of the convention bureau of a major metropolitan city. She told me she attended a party where a psychic was doing readings. She said the psychic caught her completely off guard, because she "didn't believe in this sort of thing." The psychic told her that she was under great stress and was considering a job change. She said only a few people knew that.

It wasn't until later that she realized that the psychic told most everyone else at the party the same thing. She said she caught on to the ruse when, after some reflection, she pieced together the fact that her city was under economic pressure. So it was logical that most of the city employees would be under some kind of financial strain and would be considering a job change in the light of reduced job stability.

Dr. Ray Hyman has done considerable research in this area at the University of Oregon. In one study, he developed a list of personality traits which eighty per cent of the students considered "true" about themselves. Then another group of students rated the characteristics as "desirable" or "undesirable." Using this information, Dr. Hyman composed fake sketches where seventy-five per cent of each sketch was desirable traits and twenty-five per cent was undesirable traits. He found that this mix was the most believable ratio because the undesirable traits had the effect of making the spiel more plausible.

Skilled readers will tailor their stock sketches to the community or social status of their clients in a similar, although unscientific manner.

The Barnum effect, alluding to the master showman P.T. Barnum, refers to the fact that the appeal of these stock statements is so strong that people will actually select a Barnum-type statement *over* an accurate psychological profile of themselves. This has been demonstrated in a number of tests. Dr. Hyman relates the results of one such test.

Sundberg (1955), for example, gave the Minnesota Multiphasic Personality Inventory (known as the MMPI) to 44 students. . . . The MMPI is the most carefully standardized personality inventory in the psychologist's tool kit. Two psychologists, highly experienced in interpreting the outcome of the MMPI, wrote a personality sketch for each student on the basis of his or her test results. Each student then received two personality sketches—the one actually written for him or her and a fake sketch. When asked to pick which sketch actually described him or her better, 26 of the 44 students (59 percent) picked the fake sketch![4]

In another study by Dr. Hyman, we see how important context is when one hears a fake sketch.

We gave some students a fake sketch (the third stock spiel previously discussed) and told half of them that it was the result of an astrological reading and the other half that it was the result of a new test, the Harvard Basic Personality Profile. In those days, unlike today, students had a low opinion of astrology. All the students rated each of the individual statements. But when asked to rate the sketch as a whole, the group that thought it came from an accepted personality test rated the *acceptability* significantly higher than did the group that thought it came from an astrologer. From talking to individual students it was clear that those who were in the personality-test group believed that they had received a highly accurate and unique characterization of themselves. Those in the astrology group admitted that the individual statements were applicable to themselves but dismissed the apparent success of the astrologer as due to the fact that the statements were so general that they would fit anyone. In other words, by changing the context in which they got the statements we were able to manipulate the subjects's perceptions as to whether the statements were generalities that applied to everyone or were specific characterizations of themselves.[5]

When I was on the Detroit talk show, I read to the live audience January's horoscope for that day from the local newspaper. I didn't tell the audience what month's horoscope I was reading. It said something like, "You are struggling with some unexpected financial pressures. Persevere and it will soon be behind you."

I asked, "To how many of you does this apply?" About half the audience raised their hands. Most people have some kind of financial pressure, and it is usually unexpected. Nobody plans to have cash flow problems.

"Now how many of you were born in January?" Only about twenty per cent of the raised hands stayed up.

"This means that most of you were either born in the wrong month or today's reading can't be trusted," I added amidst the self-directed laughter.

When a proficient reader mixes in stock remarks with a specific piece of information—like someone's name—the stock remarks that do relate to the person take on the illusion that they are also specific statements.

What is important to note is that with a skilled reader, it is hard to tell when their rap is stock or is actually something that they picked up on. By mixing the two—stock stuff and perceived information—a baffling mental illusion is created. Later, we'll find out how the reader states specific information that is seemingly impossible to know.

While many readers don't take the time to tailor their stock remarks, others do, and they are the successful ones. It enables their success rate to go up which in turn increases their credibility. Nothing is stronger than telling somebody something intimate and personal—particularly when that piece of information relates to something that person has struggled with unsuccessfully. Then the person can be left open to long-term counseling and manipulation by the reader.

2. Identifying the Psychological Profile

If the reader can partially pinpoint one's personality type, then it is possible to know the client's likely strengths and weaknesses. A stock sketch can then be applied using some form of a personality wheel. For instance, one such tool divides people into categories represented by four basic personality types: choleric, sanguine, phlegmatic and melancholy. An oversimplification of each is as follows:

Choleric—The pull-'em-up-by-the-boot-straps type; the president of a company or a sergeant in the army; aggressive, insensitive and hard to deter.

Sanguine—The spunky, gabby type who everyone sees as the hit of the party; is often overweight, in sales and needs to work on self-control.

Phlegmatic—This one's an accountant; calm, but slow and plodding; is detail-oriented and probably needs to clean out those drawers and throw away those files from 15 years ago.

Melancholic—The gifted and talented art director who is moody and needs a bright and cheerful spouse, an encouraging boss or they become mopey and insecure.

No one has all of the qualities of a given quadrant. Most of us are a mixture of these personality types. The wheel only shows the inherent strengths and weaknesses in each temperament that can surface. But once you hone in on at least the dominant quadrant, you can have a field day. While not scientific, because people change and react differently under different situations, the wheel is a good compass to point the direction to how someone is likely to respond in a given situation.

For example, you wouldn't take someone with a sanguine temperament and try and make him a bookkeeper, anymore than you would take a doctor with a melancholic temperament and a deep compassion for people and make him the president of a road construction company.

Many readers may not have consciously studied these characteristics, but the naturally observant person can deduce them through common sense. When a reader uses a stock profile correctly, it can be very convincing to the "mark" (client). With some practice, it isn't difficult to correctly peg a person in less than a minute or two during the stock delivery.

One might start with something that can apply to anyone like, "you have a strong desire to be respected," and then move to something more risky like: "You're quite creative, aren't you?" If the answer is no—and there will be a response that is either verbal or nonverbal (which will be covered later)—the person probably isn't a melancholic. But a sharp reader can quickly recover so as not to appear to have missed, by saying something like, "That's okay, because in your work you are the glue that holds the office together when things get tense. This is because you work pretty well under pressure," focusing on the strengths of the choleric and phlegmatic.

One doesn't have to fish for the traits of a spunky sanguine because they are the easiest to spot from the outset. And if a person has a "poker face" or an unresponsive personality, it can suggest depression, skepticism, lack of emotion or an iron will to suppress emotion.

A psychiatrist friend told me that after he went through his first hundred patients, he never saw a new problem. He only saw variations on the old ones. He said, "If I can pick up on just a little bit of the person's temperament, then, with a high degree of accuracy, I can predict their likes and dislikes, how they were raised, and how they are most likely to respond to problems."

One significant difference between my psychiatrist friend and the reader is that the patient knows *why* the counselor knows what he knows. When one sees a reader one is deceived as to how information is accessed. The foundation of the relationship is rooted in deception. When counseling is based upon prolonged deception, the client becomes increasingly dependent.

The next principle helps the reader hone down the tailored sketch to the right psychological profile and can even reveal specific information.

3. Physical Observation and Micro-expressions

Readers look for clues that can be detected primarily by three senses: touch, sight and hearing. (The sense of taste is of little value, and the sense of smell is only an effective tool when cologne and perfume, or the lack of it and a good shower, are in play.)

Touch. The sense of touch is commonly used by the palm reader. The lines in the palm are just a vehicle for the stock sketches—an inconsequential object toward which the reader's remarks are directed. What the reader feels for are uncontrollable muscle movements in the hand elicited in response to specific statements. These muscle responses are called ideomotor action.

Sometimes when the reader "hits" something that is sensitive to the mark—it can be either painful or joyous—there will be a minuscule twitch in the hand. Not everyone responds in this manner, but if a pattern develops, it can be helpful in testing exploratory remarks or detecting a direct hit.

A common practice by psychics who don't read palms is to place one of their hands on the client's hands which are resting on the table. This effects a nonverbal display of empathy and also provides an avenue for receiving tactile impressions.

A rarely displayed demonstration by modern magicians is to have an object hidden in a room, an auditorium or even in a building or city and locate it by what is called muscle reading. This is a learned skill in which the performer takes a person, who knows the location of the hidden object, by the hand or has him hold the end of a handkerchief, and locates the object.

Several performers have built a reputation for locating objects by feeling the response of the hand as they walk around searching for the concealed object. Without giving away the whole secret, success in part depends on feeling the resistance or yielding of the spectator's hand. Resistance indicates the wrong direction and yielding indicates the right direction. The resistance or the lack of it is an unconscious action on the part of the spectator.

In a similar manner, psychics "listen" to signpost muscular reactions that lead them to the answers their clients are seeking.

Hearing. The most obvious audio clue is when clients say something out loud which they later don't recall. They forget that they've said it because the reader shrewdly ignores the remark. The reader later mentions this information as if for the first time. For instance, let's say that the "client" has been identified as having a phlegmatic personality. Here is how something might leak out.

"I know you are pretty easy going, but I can see that you can be selfish. As a matter of fact, your selfishness is one reason you and your sister aren't closer than you should be," says the reader.

"That must be Janet," injects the client, engrossed in the reading.

"But your selfishness is probably a greater hindrance to you at work," the reader smoothly continues, "and that's why people are sometimes suspicious of you."

Notice that the reader shifts to another area of the person's life, deflecting attention away from the unconscious mention of the sister's name. Janet's name might not be brought up again until the end of the session or better yet, two or three readings later after a significant lapse of time.

At that point, the disclosure of Janet's name will be even more effective if revealed with another piece of information secured before or during the reading. Or the name "Janet" might accompany an educated guess concerning some other area of life so that if the guess is inaccurate, Janet's name will stun the "mark," taking the heat off the miss. Remember, this all moves along and shifts quickly, making it difficult for the client to later reconstruct.

A change of breathing is another good audio clue. When a hit is made on a personal matter, like the loss of a child, this response can surface. Prolonged steady breathing, however, can betray a lack of interest because one is off the path.

Every month I glean several trade publications for magicians only. My favorite section is the advertisements for new tricks. Sometimes the tricks live up to the copy in the ads and sometimes they don't. One such announcement might read: "Imagine that you call someone on the phone and ask them to think of any card in the deck. Then, without hidden electronic gadgetry, gimmicks, assistance from a confederate, mathematics or asking for any further information—you name the mentally selected card. Best of all, it can be repeated. Price: $250.00. All sales final."

I would skeptically read the ad, put it down, and then make a few calls to some colleagues to find out if they have seen it performed. It sounds too perfect—the stuff of a good rip-off.

Well, by accident, I innovated this very trick a few years ago; and while it isn't perfect, it works often enough and is so effective that it compensates for the few times it does fail. It hinges on the reverse of how a psychic receives information from his or her client and relies on the spectator picking up on something *I've* said.

The secret? I subliminally plant the name of a card in their mind. How? By quickly saying the name of the card at a high speed in the middle of a sentence. It is a knack I have developed, and I am rarely caught. I used this on Jon Racherbaumer, my accomplished magician friend from New Orleans, during one of our many long-distance sessions on the telephone.

During our conversation, I said, "Four-o'-clubs," almost a dozen times in a couple of minutes. I did this by quickly slurring my words as if I was pausing and saying "uh," and then continuing with the rest of the sentence. This took place while I shared with Jon another card trick I was working on at the time. I knew that he would be listening carefully to me as I relayed the instructions for the card trick we were discussing, while at the same time, he *wouldn't* be listening for anything else.

Then I said, "Think of a card. Now, find it and remove it from the deck," which he did, several hundred miles away from me.

"Why did you think of the Four of Clubs?" I asked.

Jon was overwhelmed. Then while he was pumping me for how I did it—he suspected it was simply a lucky guess—I injected another card: "Two-o'-hearts," several times into my dialogue. I successfully repeated the same trick three times on one of the best magicians in the world—without detection. You don't have to be successful more than one out of every two or three times to impress someone. The concept is the same as the old subliminal flashing of the popcorn frame in the movie to increase sales.

In another context, this could be a subversive tool that a reader could use to subliminally control a client—a device where an emotionally stable or unstable person seeking help would have no idea how or from where certain thoughts originated.

Sight. Some readers like to use a prop to play off of—a palm, regular or Tarot cards, a crystal ball, or even a personal article like a ring or a lock of hair. It not only provides something to which to tie the stock sketches and "fishing expeditions," but it also furnishes a focal point for the person to look at. This helps to establish a set facial position so that micro-expressions are more easily recognized.

Micro-expressions are minute facial gestures that we unknowingly betray. They are much like ideomotor actions, the uncontrollable muscle responses earlier described, in that they happen without the subject being aware of them.

For example, if the subject's eyelids slightly narrow, it can be a signal that the reader is missing the mark or is touching on something that is sensitive. If the eyelids open wider, one is usually on target or is touching on an area of interest to the client. That's why it's beneficial to the reader for the subject to be focused on some object. It helps establish a facial pattern in the client's face, so that when there is a micro-expression, it can be more easily discerned.

The ABC news magazine, *20/20,* did a story about a consultant group that has amassed a large volume of research regarding micro-expressions. A demonstration was taped where participants had to answer questions while watching a gruesome surgical operation. The participants were told to lie when answering the questions. One of the questions asked was, "Do you find this pleasant?" Each had to lie and respond, "Yes." Without training, one would never know that they were lying, but close-ups of the faces revealed their true thoughts.

The inside edge of one woman's eyebrows minutely slanted upward, only for a brief moment. The movement was slight and betrayed sadness or remorse. Only about ten per cent of the population can do this voluntarily. This fleeting action betrayed her real emotions. She did not find the operation pleasant. The reaction of the correspondent was different. He clenched his teeth when he tried to lie which minutely flexed his masseter muscle in his jaw, betraying a release of tension.

Because people can falsely portray what they are really thinking, the observation of facial expressions is not a flawless map to tell us what one is thinking. If one were familiar with the range of micro-expressions and could trigger them spontaneously, it would be difficult to evaluate what someone was thinking solely based upon facial changes. But most people who go to a reader do not have this kind of information or physical ability, giving the reader a potent edge.

Again, it should be pointed out that most psychics are not formally schooled in such things as micro-expressions, but they do keep an intuitive mental file of what works. Many psychics subliminally pick up information and use it without even knowing they are reading micro-expressions. When this happens, some begin to believe their own deceptions.

Clothes, body posture, tilt of head, positioning of hands all telegraph something. Dr. Hyman cites an example of how much can be gleaned by just observing attire.

A young lady in her late twenties or early thirties visited a character reader. She was wearing expensive jewelry, a wedding band, and a black dress of cheap material. The observant reader noted that she was wearing shoes which were currently being advertised for people with foot trouble.

By means of just these observations, the reader proceeded to amaze his client with his insights. He assumed that this client came to see him, as did most of his female customers, because of a love or financial problem. The black dress and the wedding band led him to reason that her husband had died recently. The expensive jewelry suggested that she had been financially comfortable during marriage, but the cheap dress indicated that her husband's death had left her penniless. The therapeutic shoes signified that she was now standing on her feet more than she was used to, implying that she was working to support herself since her husband's death.

The reader's shrewdness led him to the following conclusion—which turned out to be correct: The lady had met a man who had proposed to her. She wanted to marry the man to end her economic hardship. But she felt guilty about marrying so soon after her husband's death. The reader told her what she had come to hear—that it was all right to marry without further delay.[6]

This example merely demonstrates good detective work and not a psychic or supernatural gift.

To demonstrate this for a group of college students, I had a young married woman think of a problem which was specifically important to her at the moment. I asked her to sit in a chair across from me, relax and mentally focus on her problem.

Earlier I noticed her picking at some dried spots of latex paint on her fingers, so I said, "You are thinking of a problem you are having at home," to which she nodded.

"You are trying to figure out how you are going to get your kitchen or bedroom decorated before company comes—yours or your husband's parents, . . . isn't that correct?" Nodding, her eyes widened with fright. "I can't believe it," she said. "How did you know?"

The process was fairly simple. She was neatly dressed, so I took a chance that the paint meant that she was probably in a hurry to attend the lecture and didn't have time to thoroughly clean her hands. Her immaculate attire gave rise to this conclusion. I started with a material versus a personal problem because her retiring personality precluded her sharing something intimate in front of a group of strangers. So I chased the paint clue.

I speculated that she was doing some personal redecoration under a time crunch and that the time pressure related to her problem.

Most young homemakers, if given a choice, will want to decorate the kitchen or bedroom first. Parents or in-laws are always high on the list to impress, and one never gets one's objectives done on time.

By carefully timing my remarks and pausing to observe any microexpressions, including movement of her hands—I was holding her hands, palm-down, at my fingertips—I could cover my tracks if I missed on a particular point. Experience took over from there. With time you don't consciously think of each and every point, but let your training take over.

In another example, when I spoke to a group of executives, I had several men each think of a simple geometric symbol from a group I flashed at them. I then told them that I would watch their reactions as I held each symbol up and then state which symbol each mentally selected. The first symbol I held up was a circle.

One of the men slightly raised his eyebrows hoping to falsely lead me astray. I told him that although he wanted me to select him, he didn't think of the circle. He then adopted a more placid expression. When I held up the square, after flashing two other symbols, I saw the masseter muscle in his jaw slightly bulge. As I handed him the square, I explained that this is often a subtle clue of a release of nervous energy. He was trying to maintain perfect composure, but couldn't quite maintain it. My percentage guess was correct.

Looking at the three hundred assembled, I drolly confirmed what they wanted to ask. "Yes, it can be used during a negotiation, and no I have not yet turned it to my financial advantage."

4. Accessing Specific Information

On the surface this principle seems obvious like the others, but the techniques used are not. Acquiring useful information can take place before, during, or after a reading, and every successful reader has his or her own pet methods.

Eavesdropping. When I was in college doing shows to earn extra money, I would go in the men's restroom prior to the performance and sit in one of the stalls with the stall door closed. I waited until I heard a couple of men discussing something that would be of use later, like a piece of information relating to a business transaction. Next, I would note what color shoes they were wearing, follow them out and then match the voice with the shoes.

Then during the show, I would have the person come up, select a card and then say, "I want you to concentrate on your card. Oh, by the way, that deal on Jackson Blvd.? Don't worry about it. The bank will come through." Without confirming or denying my spontaneous remark, his reaction confirmed for the audience that I knew what he was thinking. It created the illusion that no thought was concealed from me. It didn't take long, however, before I dropped this as a part of my presentation. The risk was too great that I might leak something that would actually harm the participant.

Simple Research. One ploy used by some readers to obtain information in advance of a reading is to tell a client that he or she will have to wait two or three weeks for an appointment. "A full schedule," is offered as the reason when the delay is actually to buy time for research. Informants, public records and private detectives are brought into play to do research before the first encounter. This is particularly true when the client is affluent.

Detailed Records. A log of pertinent information discussed in a reading is also useful. This data can then be incorporated into a later reading or into a reading with a completely different client, possibly a friend the first client has referred. A handful of readers actually network their information with other readers, so when a client moves to another city, the information in the file is sold to a reader in the new location. The member of this "psychic mafia" in the new city picks up where the old reader left off, further propagating the myth.

One reader, whom I know personally, evolved one of the best methods known for getting information about people. He does horoscope readings in department stores for a couple of dollars each. Picking from a large stable of stock sketches that he has custom tailored for different personality types, he provides what the store considers "harmless amusement." From these readings, he gleans a few regular clients by giving them his card. They can then later call and see him at his office where he presents a legitimate, businesslike front.

During or after the reading in the store, he tries to pick up on a specific piece of information that can be later used. This often happens when the client opens his or her wallet or purse to pay. He only gathers additional information when he has a particularly successful reading where he expects a call-back and the person looks convinced.

Next, he'll do research on that bit of information. If he sights a doctor bill, for example, he'll try and find out the type of doctor, who has an ailment and so forth. If, for instance, the doctor is an oncologist, one who treats and diagnoses cancer, this is noted and filed under the person's name.

A week later the person calls for an appointment. They are put on hold under the pretense of getting an appointment calendar. The reader looks up the card and notes that a bill was in their possession from Doctor Nobler. The odds are pretty good that the caller or someone in the immediate family has received treatment for a tumor.

The reader returns to the phone and starts to take down the information for the appointment. In the middle of making the appointment, the reader interrupts, "I don't know why, but I sense that you've got at least one concern related to you or someone in your family. You're not worried about a medical condition, are you? A tumor or something? I hope I'm not right about this."

If the answer is yes, the illusion is created that the reader knows and really cares about the person on the other end of the line. The information appears to have been given impromptu. This first question is also vague enough to encompass a number of medical conditions in the caller or someone else that they know—past, present or future.

Getting information about someone's personal or business relationships is not a difficult challenge for the persistent reader. Reporters, police, attorneys and investigative reporters do it all the time, but for legitimate purposes. With the aid of the computer, it is even easier for the enterprising reader to organize and perform data searches. By using the next principle, loading the language, the illusion of randomly tapping into concealed information can be even more convincing.

5. Loading the Language

When this technique is combined with the others already mentioned, one can give the appearance of never being wrong, even after an actual miss. Loading the language refers to statements which can be interpreted in more than one way. I have already cited two examples.

Remember how the psychic in the talk show asked the concerned mother, "Your daughter isn't detail-oriented, is she?" lilting her voice at the end? This allowed her exploratory statement to be used successfully regardless of the mother's response. If the answer was yes, the psychic would have said, "Because your daughter is detail-oriented. . . ." If the answer was no, the response would have been, "That's because she is socially oriented, and. . . ."

This is an example of an either/or phrase. Either the daughter is detail-oriented or she is socially oriented. It's not necessary that the person physically answer the statement, although most do because the reader is disarming and projects trust. When verbal answers are absent, micro-expressions will often tip the answer.

The discerning of the young wife's problem is an example of a statement that covers a broad range of subjects. "You are thinking of a problem you are having at home . . ." can apply to marital, health, relative, construction or decorating problems. It's simply a matter of the reader being clever enough to turn an apparent miss into a hit by shifting the focus. If the answer is no (either verbally or non-verbally), the shift must be unnoticeable, actually interrupting the client the instant a response is detected, which will leave a lasting impression that the reader never detected a response.

The example of keying off the doctor bill is similar to the last illustration. "You're not worried about a medical condition, are you?" can either apply directly to the caller or someone they know. Most people know someone who is having a medical problem, particularly if one is thirty years of age or older.

The key to loading the language is to use an ambiguous statement in a context that makes it sound specific. It is especially effective when combined with the next principle, the educated guess.

6. The Educated Guess
This is the final component for creating the illusion of real powers during a reading. When it's used and the reader hits, it is electrifying to the unsuspecting.

During one program, I singled out a woman from the audience whom I perceived to be very outgoing and probably of a sanguine temperament. The old saying goes that opposites attract, so it was a safe guess that her husband was somewhat phlegmatic—the opposite of a sanguine temperament. In addition, males that are phlegmatic make for good accountants, engineers and architects. Because the majority of the audience were professionals, the probability was small that her husband held down a blue-collar job.

I asked the woman to tell me if I was correct in my character analysis of her husband. Quickly, I then ran off a few of the basic characteristics of the phlegmatic, watching for any telltale micro-expressions which might tell me if I was on target or not. Her eyes opened slightly wider during the character reading, which confirmed that I was in the ball park. I concluded, "And your husband is probably an accountant, . . ." deliberately not finishing my sentence. She nodded in agreement.

I didn't complete my sentence, so that if I perceived a negative response, I would have finished, "or an engineer," as engineers are more common than architects (a profession which also attracts those with a phlegmatic temperament). With proper timing and hitting on the second guess, this technique can cover for an apparent miss.

Good educated guesses are based on percentages, like the use of names. The most common report I hear is something like this, "But he told me the name of my father who died fifteen years ago." There are many possible tacks to get the job done. Here is one.

The reader first makes a guess with a common name like Bill or Mary. Let's say that the reader gets a negative response to a question like, "Does the name Mary mean anything to you? She appears to be having some physical or emotional problems and you are the person that can help her." If the answer is no (through either a verbal response or a micro-expression), the psychic might respond, "Well, watch for someone named Mary. I'm sure that this person will have some significant meaning for you in the near future. And yes, [dramatic pause] she will have brown hair. Yes, I'm sure of it."

The language has been loaded and the option of meeting Mary in the future is added. It's a high percentage guess. It can also set the stage for a self-fulfilling prophecy. The client will now make it his or her business to keep a lookout for a brunette named Mary. Remember, the reader doesn't have to hit every time. A twenty or thirty per cent accuracy rate is all that's needed to develop a reputation. If the reader does hit on the first guess, micro-expressions can then be used to physically describe the person and their relationship to the client. When the other components of a reading lock up with a good guess, it really looks like a gift from another world.

When a reader is on a roll and has had two or three strong hits during a reading, it is not uncommon to go further out on a limb and make a smaller percentage guess. If the guess involves a name, for example, Stanley—a not so common name—might be tossed out. Even if the reader is wrong, this will not discourage the client from making it fit in the future because credibility has been established in the client's mind by the previous hits. Dates, initials, types of businesses, personal problems can all be handled in the same manner.

Techniques Multiply the Applications

You see, even if one knows all the *principles,* no one can ever know all the *techniques* by which the principles can be applied because more often than not, the techniques are invented by the psychic as a matter of necessity and changing conditions.

If confronted by someone trying to convince you of his or her psychic powers that you can't immediately explain, back off. Ask yourself questions like: Why is the person doing this? What does he or she stand to gain? Can any of the principles of a cold reading even be remotely applied? If still stymied, call someone you trust to help you check out the facts, someone with a better grasp of the principles.

Powers of State Meet Powers of Stars

When I lectured and presented demonstrations of cold reading for the student body of Dartmouth College in May of 1988, there was great laughter when I made reference to President Reagan's former chief of staff Don Regan's disclosure earlier that month that Mrs. Reagan had actively consulted a San Francisco astrologer. Later reports confirm that the astrologer was actually Joan Quigley. Vassar-educated and the daughter of hotelier magnate John Quigley, the sixty-plus-year-old Quigley was introduced to Nancy Reagan in the early seventies. In his book *For the Record,* Regan detailed the extraordinary influence that Quigley wielded via Mrs. Reagan.

According to Regan, Mrs. Reagan "seemed to have absolute faith" in Quigley's clairvoyant powers. Mrs. Reagan became a believer after Quigley told her that "something bad" (loading the language here?) was going to happen to the president, her husband, shortly before the 1981 assassination attempt by John Hinckley which almost took his life.

For several years Quigley's prognostications affected when press conferences would or would not be held; the precise day, October 9, 1986, when the president would leave for the Reykjavik, Iceland, nuclear-arms summit with Mikhail Gorbachev (the First Lady opted not to go after consultation with Quigley); and the decision concerning when a large polyp was to be removed from the president's large intestine. These and many other decisions first went through Quigley's astral channels. The predictions had become such a "factor" in Regan's work that he had to keep a color-coded calendar for good (green), bad (red) and "iffy" (yellow) days—marked like a celestial traffic light. Quigley's influence was alarming. Regan writes:

> But the President's schedule is the single most potent tool in the White House, because it determines what the most powerful man in the world is going to do and when he is going to do it. By humoring Mrs. Reagan we have given her this tool—or, more accurately, gave it to an unknown woman in San Francisco who believed that the zodiac controls events and human behavior and that she could read the secrets of the future in the movements of the planets.[7]

To what extent the president himself trusts in astrology is unclear. On May 17, 1988, following the disclosure, he said, "I've not tied my life by it . . . but I don't know enough about it to say, is there something to it or not."[8] What is clear is that Quigley through Mrs. Reagan affected the day-to-day operation of the White House.

This is not unique in history. Nostradamus guided the paths of Henry

II and Catherine of Medici in the middle 1500s, and Rasputin, the crazed monk, directed decisions of Nicholas II, the last Czar of All the Russias, and his wife Czarina Alexandra. Today there are many in key government and corporate positions of influence who are following the same path. How does this happen? One reason is that the seekers are getting information that is "perceived" to be accurate.

I pointed out to the Dartmouth Ivy Leaguers that in fifteen years of investigations I had never met a successful psychic who could accurately give specific information over a sustained period of time without using, knowingly or unknowingly, cold reading. Their laughter at Mrs. Reagan's faux pas was stopped cold in its tracks when I followed up my observations by "reading the minds" of some bewildered students. Those in their seats soberly heeded the buyer-beware sign that I posted that warned that almost anyone can be taken given the proper context. Usually, the more intelligent the client the more confusing the deception, because there is more cerebral stuff in which to layer the deception.

Threat to State Secrets

Lost in the editorial cartoons and backroom jokes directed at the Regan disclosure was the fact that state secrets may have been compromised. First, because it is not certain that the First Lady's conversations with Quigley were over secured telephone lines, and more important, that Quigley was not knowingly or unknowingly pumping Mrs. Reagan for information and adding it to her pool from her other clients.

Think about it. If Mrs. Reagan and other individuals like her in key government and corporate positions aren't getting accurate information—past, present or future—they wouldn't keep coming back to the Joan Quigleys for advice. These clients are often savvy folks who can rule out chance and self-fulfilling prophecies. It's the accurate information delivered with beguiling charm that knocks them for a loop.

Remember the adept reader never uses these principles in an isolated state; they are always interwoven. Experience shows that over sixty per cent of the population will state that the reader must be using a psychic or supernatural power when accurate—this in defiance of any socioeconomic demographic.

The packaging for the readings in the Quigley case is astrology. Is there anything to it? All scientific testing over the past several decades delivers a resounding no. Today, astrologers fall into two broad camps: one group predicts the future; a second group does character readings offering personal counseling. Under unbiased testing both fall flat on their charts when it comes to accuracy.

To see if astrologers can predict the future we simply have to study their track record. Studies show they are accurate less than ten per cent of the time (and most of the accurate predictions are so general that they are not considered specific: for example, "government spending will increase next year").

The character or personal reading is also easily put to the test. When astrologers are asked to examine charts that are prepared according to the disciplines of astrology as well as bogus charts—charts that are simply made up—testing shows that astrologers can't tell the difference between the two. They can't tell the difference between the bogus chart and the chart drawn up according to their own disciplines. In addition, to flush out those using cold reading—and most do—a scenario like the one I used in Detroit will expose the real story.

One clever aspect of astrology is the convoluted complexity involved in professionally drawing up a chart. It can take up to a year just to learn the trade. It is not surprising, then, when a small minority of astrologers really believe that the system works when they unwittingly use some of the principles of cold reading when interpreting the chart for a client. It is during the interpretation phase that the astrologer directly interacts with the client. This is done to help the client understand their chart in relationship to their personal life. When testing is set up, however, to eliminate the cold-reading factor, we find that the charts are valueless. (In a follow-up to this book, a more detailed discussion of astrology will be presented.)

These indictments even come from astrologers themselves. John Townley, a noted and respected (in his own ranks) astrologer, wrote:

I would say that most of the accusers of astrology are probably correct. They think that astrology are 100-percent charlatans, but I would bring it down to 90 percent. Not necessarily even intentional charlatans. But . . . they are suffering from the same failing. Maybe 50 percent of the people out there are deliberately selling hokum straight ahead.[9]

In all the years that I have followed up countless cases where intelligent people were convinced that a reader had a power or gift based upon what they had experienced, I have never found a psychic, gypsy fortune-teller or channeler who was the real McCoy. But, if their claims can't be verified, then how do they gain recognition and community acceptance?

Part II
Psychic Detectives

Chapter 4

Examining Two Prominent Psychic Detectives

MOST COMMONLY WE HEAR OF PSYCHICS IN NEWSPAPERS, MAGAZINES AND ON local news broadcasts. The more credible news sources, like *The New York Times*, will refer to "psychics," using quotation marks to notify the reader that there is some doubt about the claims in question.[1]

But most magazines and newspapers are not as discriminating. So the exploits of psychics are usually reported without in-depth research into the facts of a case or any follow-up stories when the psychic fails. The reporter from the Associated Press who did the initial story on James Hydrick, the psychic I exposed in "Psychic Confession," is a good example of this kind of reporting, leading readers to believe that these people really do have powers.

Flyers placed on car windshields and delivered to home doorsteps, personal ads in local newspapers and television guides, coupons in savings books and even slick billboards are all used by those claiming powers to hook us. A friend of mine—at the time a president of a chemical company—even received a mailer geared toward the executive.

Society parties are another outlet for exposure. Here contacts can be made with those with large sums of money. Company and community functions are another outlet. Recently a well-known mental health organization hired psychics to do readings at their annual fund raiser. Here an organization committed to mental health was unwittingly contributing to the problem they want to solve!

And, as mentioned earlier, psychic fairs are held in hotels and convention halls in most major cities. Open to the public for a charge of usually $5.00, one then pays another $5.00 to $15.00 per reading. At one fair, I shot footage of a booth manned and sponsored by the Boy Scouts of America. Where is the discernment, if not for ourselves, for our children?

Newspaper Headlines

But by far, the most spectacular hook of the psychic trade are the psychic detectives. Even those skeptical of psychics who do readings are impressed by sensational headlines, bannering the cases allegedly solved by the psychic detective.

☐ *Psychic Has Helped Solve 13 Murders*—Tampa, Florida.
☐ *Woman Claims Psychic Vision of Paperboy*—Des Moines, Iowa.
☐ *Psychic's Help Sought to Find Missing Girl*—Beaumont, Texas.
☐ *Dallas Psychics Work on Murder Cases*—Dallas, Texas.
☐ *Jersey 'Psychic' Searches Atlanta for Killer of Children*—New York City.

Local law enforcement agencies spend countless hours each year following the leads of self-described psychic detectives.

In Atlanta in 1980, a rash of nineteen slayings of black youths made national headlines. A famous New Jersey psychic was brought in to help solve the crimes. In a Dallas case involving a missing child who was later found alive and safe after being abducted, the mother was asked why she called in the psychics. She said, "I'm normally not into this stuff, [but] this is not a time to question what you believe in." In these two cases and in the ones cited by the headlines, the psychics were not successful in aiding police efforts with their "powers."

L.A.P.D. Study

The Los Angeles Police Department decided to find out if psychics can be useful in criminal investigations. Two scientific studies were conducted in 1978 and 1980 by Dr. Martin Reiser, director of behavioral studies for the L.A.P.D.

Each study was "double blind," meaning that neither the psychics nor their questioners were given any information about the homicide cases in question. The psychics simply were given objects to hold—objects that were worn or owned by the deceased (a common request by psychics)—and asked to give their impressions. In the 1978 study, only psychics were tested. In the 1980 study, a group of police detectives and a group of nonpsychic college students were tested. The observations of the test groups were recorded, then compared with the facts of the four homicide cases in question. (Two of the homicides had already been solved; two were still under investigation.)

Dr. Reiser states that, "The psychics were not able, beyond a level of chance, to come up with information that was useful. We had some who would tell us something we already knew. They'd say, 'I see a church, a churchyard, or someone killed in a churchyard.' Well, we already knew that. It was not investigatively useful. Other people might be impressed by that, but we're not. The bottom line was that they all did very, very poorly in giving information that was of investigative usefulness. We do not use psychics because we do not find them cost-effective."[2]

A similar study was done in 1984 at KUSA television in Denver. Their investigative team came up with the same conclusions.

What about the Reported Successes?

Although psychics usually accept no fees in a criminal investigation, the publicity they receive translates into increased credibility, clientele and higher fees. So you're probably thinking, "But what about all the news accounts where they *do* solve crimes?" The question is: Do they really solve crimes?

In every case that I have followed up where psychics claim they have helped local police, the evidence points to the same conclusion reached in the study by the Los Angeles Police Department.

Examining the Atlanta case, the psychic in question never provided one shred of evidence. The national press covered her entry into the case, but never reported that she proved useless and was actually an embarrassment to the Atlanta Police Department.

I personally intervened in a case where a family of five disappeared on February 14, 1981—Valentine's Day—while on a boat outing on Lake Dallas, north of Dallas. Foul play was suspected because the weather did not appear to be a factor.

A Dallas-area psychic, John Catchings, was called in out of desperation by officer Don Smith of the Lake Dallas Police Department. He called Catchings because he had heard that Catchings had helped several Texas law enforcement agencies. Catchings is one of the best-known psychic detectives in the country. I called the police chief, Y. G. Carr, and told him that I did not believe Catchings had any powers and that he was just looking for publicity. He agreed and said, "I know the guy doesn't have any powers, and I wish our officer had never called that Catchings fellow."

The local press had a field day with the story, showing Catchings flying over the area in a local news station's helicopter. The results? He *missed on every clue* he gave police, but the myth was propagated that he did provide positive assistance. Again, as in most cases, the local press didn't follow up on his failures. The net result was that people remembered the headline stating that he was brought into the case.

Virtually every law enforcement officer and reporter I have interviewed admits that Catchings has no powers. I asked one officer how Catchings seemed to hit on one clue in a case involving the disappearance of an attractive young woman. He said that Catchings *was given* that information in confidence by the police, and he leaked it to the press. The officer kept quiet, not wanting to explain how stupidly the information was divulged.

Consider another case reported in the *Dallas Morning News*, April 29, 1984.

Sgt. L. C. Stinett of the Maryland State Police worked with Dallas psychic John Catchings in the unsolved murder case of Mary Cook Spencer who disappeared from her Lusby, Md., home in 1981. At the request of Mrs. Spencer's parents, Catchings traveled to Maryland a year ago to help search for her body. He has since brought in his "psychic detective squad" for help in the case.

Stinett says he appreciated Catchings's visit, but he doesn't believe Catchings has any powers.

"I think that by him being in the area, one thing we gained was we were allowed to perform an additional search of the area, which may not have been allowed without him coming," Stinett says. "But as far as them having psychic ability, I don't believe in that bunk. I believe they do no more than use good common sense, good logic.

"I've never seen a psychic go out on a case without previously going over the case and having knowledge of the case," Stinett say. "I think some of them are very intelligent and would make very good police detectives. But I don't think they have psychic ability any more than you or I have.

"Some of them are complete hoaxes. Some of them send someone in advance to pick up little tidbits on the case that they can drop later. Now, John Catchings didn't do that."

Despite his skepticism, Stinett allows that he picked up some pointers when he observed Catchings as he led law enforcement officers in a search of the area where they believe the body may have been buried.

"Whenever there was a low spot or a high spot in the woods, he directed us to dig," Stinett says. "One of the things he taught us is that when somebody buries a body, you have to do something with the ground to hide it. If it's a recent burial, the ground will be disturbed. If it's old, the ground will sink. Also, it's hard to put leaves and sticks over the grave to make the ground look normal. So you will have a pile of brush over the grave or a pile of trash. That's what I learned from John Catchings."

Police will sometimes use a psychic as a gimmick to gain attention so they can reopen or solve a case. In the Maryland case, that's what Stinett did.

In another homicide case not related to Catchings, the police invented the story that a psychic had provided the necessary clues. The reason for the fabricated story was to conceal the actual source: a former cell mate of the murderer was the tip and the psychic cover story was used to protect the identity of the cell mate.

Now, ask yourself this question. If psychics can really solve crimes, why don't the FBI and CIA use them? Why are they only brought in by an emotionally distraught family or an officer without leads who, out of desperation, convinces his superior to let the psychic have a shot? Tens of thousands of hours of valuable police time have been wasted running down psychic leads. One might think this is humorous until you take the time to sit down with the families of the victims who need real hope coupled with legitimate action.

Finding a Missing Body

Dr. Marcello Truzzi, professor of sociology at Eastern Michigan University, sent me an excellent report by Ward Lucas, an investigative journalist with twenty years of experience. After years of searching, Lucas, an investigative reporter at KUSA in Denver, thought he found a bona fide report from police accounts in which a psychic, Greta Alexander, in Alton, Illinois, actually helped to find the skeletal remains of a twenty-eight-year-old female, missing for five months. The following account appeared in the *Campus Law Enforcement Journal* in August of 1985.

Police firmly believed they had solved the case. They had strong evidence that pointed to the boyfriend of the missing woman as the killer. But Mary Cousett had been missing for five months and, without the body, a criminal case would be hard to bring to trial. All this was conveyed to Greta Alexander. The psychic's brow furrowed as she melted into her customary trance. After a few intense moments, visual images began to form. Pictures. Vibrations. A road that forks. A bridge. A church. Piles of gravel. As the images poured forth, Sergeant William Fitzgerald took notes on a small pad. A Madison County Map was produced by another officer and given to Greta. "Where is the body?" someone asked excitedly. "Can you see it?"

Greta Alexander sighed deeply and the pencil quivered. "I feel it . . . right . . . there!" Her extended arm drew a small circle on the map next to the Mackinaw River.

"I know the place!" another officer said. "It's on Route 121."

The searchers were on the scene a short time later thrashing through the knee-high brush that the November winds had stripped of their summer foliage. The police officers knew this area well, because they'd searched it on prior occasions while looking for the missing body. But this search was different. Within three hours, police officer Steve Trew called out to the others. He had spotted a bit of clothing . . . then some hair . . . and the scattered bones. Mary Cousett's body had been located!

This is how most people would hear the story. But the full list of the psychic's clues were even more extensive. See if you can spot how many different principles of cold reading appear in the list.

1. The area where the body is found has already been searched.
2. A man with funny-looking boots walked right past the body during a previous search.

3. The man with the boots had a dog.

4. A man with a crippled hand will find the body.

5. There are three roads.

6. The initial "S" will play an important role.

7. The initial "B" is around the victim's body.

8. The body would not be found in the state where she was born.

9. Grabner's farm would play a part.

10. There would be tree cuttings near the body.

11. The road splits near the body.

12. The road near the body is bumpy.

13. The body will be off the main highway.

14. A leg or a foot on the body will be missing.

15. The head will not be with the body.

16. The body will be near a bridge.

17. The body was dragged from the place where the victim was killed.

18. Only part of the body will be showing.

19. Cars stopping nearby will be important.

20. The body will be down an embankment.

21. A faded sign will be important.

22. The body will be across a road, down from the river.

23. Piles of salt or rock on the highway nearby will be important.

24. A church will play an important part.

A Closer Look

On the surface, this reads pretty impressively. But Lucas was not so easily taken in. He continued his report by saying:

Keeping in mind that Alexander [the psychic] is from the area, and has worked with police investigators in the past, we must assume she knew a few things about murder cases in general and this case in particular.

In fact, Sergeant Fitzgerald confirmed that police had told Ms. Alexander they had good reason to believe the victim's body had been left along Highway 121 next to the Mackinaw river. Police had searched the banks of the river many times without success, and they let her know this as well!

What follows is Lucas's analysis of each prediction. My additional comments appear in brackets.

1. *Area already searched.* This is a common prediction of psychics in old cases where the mystic has been directed to a possible location. It's obvious police have used more conventional methods first.

2. *Man with funny-looking boots.* They're searching a riverbank, remember? This prediction is self-fulfilling since someone will come forward and say he was wearing boots on the day he searched the area. In fact, someone did.

3. *Man with boots had a dog.* This was a fair-chance guess, since dogs are normally used in searches of this type.

4. *Man with crippled hand will find body.* This was a fantastic psychic hit! Good show, Greta. The finder of the body did, in fact, have an injured finger!

5. *The body is near three roads.* It's common for psychics to call for things in threes. In fact, this is a pretty good self-fulfilling guess, since the officers will look down the road until they see the three streets in question. A fourth road further down is frequently ignored. [Loading the language?]

6. *The initial "S."* Self-fulfilling. Steve found the body. But "S" is the most commonly used letter in the alphabet, so this could refer to piles of "salt" on the road, or "sticks" near the body, or "scraps" of paper on the ground.

7. *The initial "B."* Same as previous point.

8. *Body not found in state where she was born.* Newspaper articles had mentioned the victim was born in Mississippi. It's a pretty good guess for a psychic to surmise the body was in Illinois, not Mississippi.

9. *Grabner's farm.* No one could confirm this.

10. *Tree cuttings.* A complete miss.

11. *Road splits.* A good odds-on guess.

12. *Road is bumpy.* This might have been a good odds-on guess, since she's dealing with three roads, but Sergeant Fitzgerald says it was a complete miss! [Also, you would expect to find the body in a more obscure area, closer to a dirt road than a paved one.]

13. *Body off main highway.* Almost meaningless prediction since "off" the highway could mean virtually any distance. [Logically if it was on or very near a main highway it probably would have been sighted.]

14. *Leg or foot missing.* Good guess, since animals almost always scatter the bones.

15. *Head not with body.* Another good guess for the same reason.

16. *Body near bridge.* Almost self-fulfilling when the body is next to a river that has many bridges. In fact, the bridge was some quarter to a half a mile away. [If a half mile can be considered "near," then this gives a one-mile spread, taking into consideration the distance on both sides of the bridge—not very precise.]

17. *The body had been dragged.* Unconfirmed.

18. *Only part of body showing.* Good odds-on guess because the psychic knew the area had already been searched.

19. *Cars stopping nearby.* A complete miss.

20. *Body down an embankment.* Good odds-on guess.

21. *Faded sign.* There are a lot of faded signs on highways, but in this case, the only sign nearby was not faded.

22. *Body is across a road down from the river.* Meaningless prediction.

23. *Piles of rock or salt.* Self-fulfilling. The officers looked until they spotted one of the many piles of salt along this stretch of highway. It was about a quarter of a mile away.

24. *Church plays a part.* Almost self-fulfilling. There was a church camp about a half mile to a mile down the road. But the use of churches is a common prediction of psychics. If a church isn't nearby, it could be the victim went to church the day before she died.

"But we're missing the biggest criticism of all," continued Lucas.

". . . When the officers came back from discovering the body, they apparently 'forgot' that the circle Greta drew on the map was nowhere near the location of the body. In fact, she missed! Completely! According to Fitzgerald, the circle was drawn over an area several miles away."

Mary Cousett's family was relieved that the ordeal was finally over. To them it was irrelevant if Alexander had psychic gifts or not. But, because of a lack of discernment in the community, the story of Alexander's psychic involvement was broadly exploited by much of the media.

When claims of psychic abilities go unchecked and are promoted in the media, a deceptive mindset begins and a healthy sense of discernment disappears. Hopefully, you now have a better handle on what you read and hear concerning these kinds of reports. Before closing this section, let's look at how cold reading is used on radio and television call-in shows.

Chapter 5

The Media Connection

EVERY MAJOR CITY HAS ITS SHARE OF PSYCHICS WHO APPEAR ON RADIO AND television talk shows. They boost ratings for profit-minded stations as people from all walks of life call in to talk to the psychics and get advice. On October 30, 1985, John Catchings appeared on the Dallas's radio station KVIL to do psychic readings and promote an upcoming psychic fair that was to be held in November. The show was the "Ron Chapman Morning Show," Dallas's top-rated broadcast. Chapman is recognized nationally as one of his industry's leading innovators.

I called Chapman's producer, Sandy Hopkins, and told her that I had followed up on many of Catchings's "psychic detective" cases. I informed her of what law enforcement officials had told me—that most didn't believe that he had any psychic abilities. I also shared with her the number of cases where people had been locally victimized by area psychics. I suggested that I appear on or after the same show and talk about the flip side of the issue. She refused, saying, "People want to believe in psychics and haunted houses, and we don't want to burst their bubble."

It was the first time that a station had denied me such a request. Most stations are eager to exploit the controversy because it increases their ratings. What I didn't know, until I later received a call from Chapman, was that KVIL had used Catchings to promote a number of highly successful cruises. Chapman, in his call to me, described his show as just "fun and games and not '60 Minutes.' "

High Ratings

A year before, I was a guest on one of the top ABC radio talk shows which regularly features psychics. Off the air I asked the host why she included so many psychics on her show even though she confessed they were all fakes.

"The ratings always jump when they're on," she explained. "People like this sort of stuff. They want someone to tell them that it's going to be okay."

What she didn't like, though, was when her city's most visible psychic offered to "cut her in" if she would refer clients or pass along useful information. Afterward, she invited me back to do another show, suggesting that I take any of the psychic readings from previous broadcasts and replay them on the air to expose the cold reading process.

Although Ron Chapman's producer declined to let me present the other side of the issue, another Dallas station did.

I recorded the readings that John Catchings did on Chapman's show on KVIL on October 30 and replayed them the following day on another local station, KCBI, along with an explanation of the principles of cold reading that Catchings used. To my knowledge, it was the first time readings of this nature had been replayed and explained on live radio.

More important than the fact that the phone lines were jammed during the show was one caller's comment: "My husband and I went to see a psychic just for fun and games. . . ." Then she related how they were manipulated by the psychic and encouraged listeners to "stay away." Many took her advice.

An Instant Replay

What follows are excerpts from the October 30 broadcast. Chapman introduced Catchings and noted that the local psychics had organized and adopted a "code of ethics." Catchings commented:

> Most psychics are pretty much skeptical of other psychics, I mean, the really good ones are because I know how hard it is for me to do what I do. And you know it's just sort of natural to think, "Well, there really are a lot of people in this business who are con artists and frauds and really aren't that good," and we're trying to kind of weed those guys out and draw a line and say here's what we'll do and what we won't do. And this is the difference between us and those other guys. We don't make claims that we can do things or have powers that other people can't do. It's just a talent that some people have like playing the piano.

But in another interview, Catchings had told a news reporter that what he did was "not normal," but that it was a "God-given talent." "If by the grace of God you have enough ability, then it will come forth some day," he added, playing off people's belief in God.

When I asked for a copy of the code of ethics from one of the heads of their organization, the request was denied. One of the purposes of the code of ethics was to cut out the gypsy fortunetellers who only belong to their own tightly knit coterie.

To distinguish himself from the frauds, Catchings claimed to have a "nine to one" accuracy ratio, yet in a newspaper account in the *Beaumont Enterprise,* February 17, 1984, he stated, "I am 20 percent flat wrong. . . . About 60 percent of the time, I am partly right. Another 20 percent I'm right." So much for accountability.

Now, you be the "psychic detective" and scrutinize the readings of one of America's better-known psychics on this particular radio show. A brief summation of the reason the caller phoned or the caller's exact words is followed by Catchings's verbatim readings. After each reading is a summation of the principles and techniques he used.

Reading One.

A postal worker called and said that she had lost some postal keys when her house burned down. They were in her purse, and she wanted to know where they were in her house, so she might locate them in the rubble.

Catchings: I think they are still there in the debris where the house was. I think they're in the bedroom area somewhere close to a closet. And they're in a very charred area. And if you went through there with a rake you'll probably find it.

Explanation: This was just an educated guess. Most women carry keys in a purse; she even said she thought they were in her purse. Now, think about it logically. What are the two areas in a home where most women put down their purse? That's right—the kitchen and the bedroom.

Result: The keys were not located by Catchings's psychic abilities.

Reading Two.

The caller lost a diamond from the setting in her ring. She wanted to know if it was in her house or her automobile.

Catchings: I think the ring is in the automobile. I think that you hung it up on something . . . some cloth or some material . . . maybe something you were wearing. I pick up a kind of plaid kind of color. I think it is on the ground in the car close to the passenger side up underneath the seat on the floor.

Explanation: Here educated guesses were combined with loading the language. Whether the stone was in the house or car was a 50-50 proposition. Catchings opted for the car and specifically under the car mat. Think of the last time you dropped something on the floor of your car and couldn't find it. It usually works its way under the seat or mat before you notice it. If the caller had seen the stone before it slid under the seat or floor mat, she wouldn't have called.

Mention of the "plaid material" was a nice touch, but he didn't say if this was the fabric of the seat or her dress. Fall is the time of year when many women wear plaid skirts. Had he hit on this detail, it would have created the illusion that he could see something not mentioned.

Result: The caller never confirmed the relevancy of the plaid material nor did she locate her stone with Catchings's help.

Reading Three.

An astute-sounding male lost a watch while eating at a local cafeteria and wanted to know where it was.

Catchings: I think that it was left at the cafeteria, but I think that it was picked up by a patron and it's gone.

Explanation: Catchings merely stated the obvious. The man no doubt went back to the restaurant as soon as he discovered that his watch was missing. When he didn't find it and no one turned it in, the obvious conclusion was that someone picked it up—probably a patron because employees usually turn in missing articles.

Reading Four.

Caller: I've made several changes in my life recently, but one that I am really concerned about is that I'm in a sales position. I need to find out if I should stay here or if it's just the change that is making me think that I need to make a career change.

Catchings: I think it's getting close to making a career change, but I don't think it's here yet. I think you should stay where you are at. I think you can wait until the first of April before making a decision. And I think that if you want to make that decision it's okay, but your job is secure where you're at.

Explanation: Here, identifying the psychological profile, loading the language and an educated guess were used. At the time of the broadcast,

Dallas had a high divorce rate. It was very likely that the changes in her life included a divorce—although Catchings didn't reference this. Most salespersons have some sanguine traits and a common weakness is a lack of self-control. The best advice one could give to a sanguine who was under stress would be to not jump to conclusions but rather to let one's personal life settle before making a rash decision about one's job.

Catchings loaded the language when giving the caller advice to insure that regardless of what happened in the future he would be correct. He stated that her job was not in jeopardy, but a decision could be made in April. If he was wrong about her job security, then it was likely that she would seek new employment by April. If she had a secure job but was not satisfied with her position, she would again probably seek new employment.

This from-the-hip advice can be harmful emotionally and psychologically if one doesn't have all the facts. The woman's job may, in fact, have been in jeopardy, in which case Catchings gave her a false sense of security. If she was desperate enough to ask a stranger for advice on the phone, she may have been desperate enough to follow that advice and effect a self-fulfilling prophecy.

The latter is a common occurrence. The client acts out what has been suggested.

Reading Five.
Caller: This is a twin question. I have a twin brother, and he's trying to start a business south of Dallas. . . . I'm supposedly going to be his manager. Do you see it working out for us—for him to open the business and for me to have a steady job?

Catchings: I feel like this is something that he really wants to do and something that he is going to do. But I pick up a lot of delays getting it off the ground, and it may be April or May before this thing gets up and moving.

Caller: Gee [slightly discouraged tone of voice]. What do you see for my husband for a job? 3/10/43 is his birthday [referring to his astrological sign].

Catchings: Well, I pick up pretty good vibrations around him—some type of employment change coming up for him very shortly in the next thirty days.

Chapman: Whoa!

Caller: That's terrific. He is, but he doesn't know whether to take the job or not. He can take the job, and we can starve with no overtime, but [he would have the option for] advancement, or we can live on overtime and he can sit on the same stool for the next twenty years.

Chapman: Sounds like to me, he's already made the decision [jovially].

Caller: Should he go for the advancement?

Catchings: I think he'll go for the advancement, and the overtime will come.

Caller: Thank you. Terrific!

Explanation: This last reading is a good example of picking up on micro-expressions on the phone and getting information during the reading combined with some percentage guessing.

Catchings started off by reaffirming what the woman already knew: her brother wanted to start a business. Any business person could predict that getting the business started would encounter delays. The caller registered discouragement in her reply and the tone of her voice when she said, "Gee," confirmed that she needed a job now. This was reinforced when she asked about her husband's job situation. There was some uncertainty in the wind or she wouldn't have even asked about it, and her earlier disappointment indicated that they needed income.

When Catchings stated there would be a job change "in the next thirty days," it sounded impressively precise, but it was just a good percentage guess and picked up her spirits. Christmas was coming when a person in need could quite likely pick up some temporary work, and if he had been interviewing for a job, the first week in January was one of the two heaviest times of the year for new employment. So, regardless of whether he took a temporary seasonal job or an interview landed him a job,

Catchings's prediction would appear to be correct.

The woman then asked about the advancement option, confirming that he had been interviewing. Catchings safely bet that he would take the job with advancement because she registered disappointment that he would "sit on the same stool for the next twenty years." If she and her husband were willing to consider the option of advancement against overtime—plus the fact that she was willing or had to work—she would no doubt sway him to pursue the job opening that offered advancement.

The "overtime will come" closing by Catchings again lifted her spirits, finishing the reading on a positive note.

Chapman's role was to mirror excitement and the mind of the listening audience. At one point he feigned skepticism when he said, "Shoot, I can do that. How do we know you're not conning me?"

Catchings then quoted his "nine to one" accuracy ratio and a number of cases in which he was supposedly successful. These went by without challenge by Chapman, who in mock fashion played the devil's advocate during Catchings's "fun and games."

The $5,000 Offer

To follow up on the October broadcast, my crew filmed the psychic fair Catchings was promoting. I printed and distributed fliers offering to pay any of the psychics assembled $5,000 if they could present a verifiable demonstration of real psychic abilities on camera: predict the future, read someone's mind, move an object and so forth. When I explained the challenge to the head of the organization, the sheets I was holding that detailed the challenge were confiscated. A big bruiser-type who falsely identified himself as being with hotel security put his hand over the lens of the camera and escorted us out of the ballroom.

I included this footage in the children's series "Kid Tricks." When kids see the footage of the psychic fair and are asked, "What are the psychics afraid of?" the kids immediately respond, "They're afraid of getting caught." If kids can catch on, there is hope for adults.

Looking back, how did Catchings get started in all this?

This was Catchings's account of what happened during a cookout on the Fourth of July in Austin, Texas, in 1969.

I walked out in front of the house and I leaned up against a car parked there while I was waiting for the steaks to finish. I wasn't wearing any shoes or any shirt. As I was leaning up against the car, there was one little old bitty black cloud up in the sky, and suddenly lightning struck the car. And it just like froze me to it.

I had an out of body experience. An astral projection experience,* if you want it in technical terms. I could see myself. I could see the car. And I could see this blue glow all around me.

I could see a friend of mine coming toward me, and I remember feeling, "If he touches me, we'll both die." After about ten or fifteen seconds the glow, the lightning went away.[2]

He went on to say that he didn't believe the lightning altered his brain cells and gave him psychic ability, but he did explain, "Following that experience, I had what you might call a 'calling,' like a minister would have. Maybe there was something else I was supposed to do with my life, some further purpose, something deeper than what I was doing."

Catchings then told remarkable stories of how he began to manifest "psychic abilities." He later rose to prominence in part due to the promotion of a Dallas radio personality, Ron Chapman.

All of this bore uncanny resemblance to another psychic I encountered, James Hydrick. Instead of Dallas the city was Salt Lake, and the radio personality who gave Hydrick prominence was Chris Corey. And while Catchings's powers began with a bolt of lightning, for Hydrick it was a Chinese mentor, Master Wu. But there was a critical difference between the two. Hydrick's feats and claims were much more spectacular than Catchings's, and he had been incarcerated for kidnaping and robbery. Let's begin where I did, with an Associated Press release dated January 1, 1981.

Editor's Note: Astral projection is an experience in which one's spirit is allegedly separated from one's body.

Part III
Love Is a Trick:
The Hydrick Case

Chapter 6

James Hydrick's Influence

O N NEW YEAR'S DAY, 1981, AN ASSOCIATED PRESS RELEASE APPEARED IN NEWS-
papers across the country touting the "mind-over-matter skills" of
James Hydrick, a twenty-one-year-old ex-con and the operator of
a martial arts studio in Salt Lake City. What follows are some
excerpts from that article reported by Verne Anderson.

Master Mind Moves Objects

Salt Lake City (AP)—James Hydrick moves pencils by pointing at
them, catches deer with his bare hands and blocks punches and finds
objects while blindfolded.

But there's more to the gentle 21-year-old ex-con than a bag of eye-
popping parlor tricks. His mind-over-matter skills are indeed amaz-

ing, but his odyssey from discarded infant to master of martial arts is downright bizarre.

Hydrick arrived in Salt Lake City last summer to set up a martial arts school based on his knowledge of Wushu Gung Fu, an ancient Chinese discipline aimed at achieving complete mental and physical self-control.

Hydrick has, at various times and always in the presence of reporters, done the following:

☐ Turned pages of telephone books from 10 feet away and moved pens, pencils, and plants and other objects by giving them hard stares.

☐ Blocked punches and found hidden coins or car keys while blindfolded.

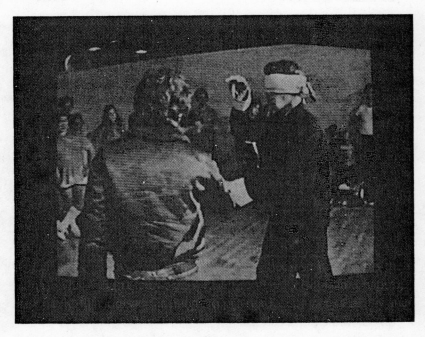

Hydrick blocking punches while blindfolded. (This picture as well as those in the following pages are taken from the video documentary "Psychic Confession.")

□ Walked blindfolded down a line of 16 people and, without touching them, known which are men and which are women.

□ Sneaked up on deer at night and grabbed them around the neck.

□ Demonstrated a level of martial arts judged by experts to be expert.

The article continued with accounts of Hydrick's life of childhood abuse, numerous foster homes, confinement in an institution for the mentally retarded, meeting Wong Chung Wu—his "mentor," and finally his arrest and incarceration related to charges of kidnapping and robbery. The article concludes:

Hydrick is eager to pass on his peculiar skills to others. Already a six-year-old pupil can move pencils and plants, he said.

"I intend to have a monastery, a temple, to train people the way of life," Hydrick said.

"The whole world has become negative," he said. "Think positive thoughts and you get positive results."

To illustrate his point, he picks up a reporter's hand, points it at a pencil and knits his brow. The pencil moves.

I mused through the story while I ate breakfast. In the background my five-year-old daughter laughed playfully as she watched the floats in the Rose Bowl Parade. I clipped the story from page thirty-four of the *Dallas Morning News* and filed it. The demonstrations sounded much like tricks I had performed as a boy, so I didn't anticipate that Hydrick would develop much of a following. I didn't expect that "thinking" people would pay much attention to it. I was wrong.

Someone in Trouble

A week later I received a call from Rob Martin, a student at Dallas Theological Seminary, a conservative evangelical school. One of the professors at the seminary, Dr. Paul Meier, a psychiatrist and founder of the noted Minirith-Meier Clinic, recommended that Rob contact me concerning his brother, Mike. Rob tentatively described to me how Mike, one of the top-ranked, professional racquetball players in the country, had fallen under the sway of James Hydrick and had subsequently experienced an emotional breakdown, apparently triggered by his relationship with Hydrick.

Mike had his breakdown while staying in the Beverly Wilshire Hotel in Los Angeles with Hydrick and some other friends while Hydrick did some television appearances. From there he was hospitalized in the psychiatric clinic at UCLA. Mike, who had a past history of emotional problems, was convinced that Hydrick had demonic powers which could be used against him. Rob, owing to his seminary training, was also convinced that Hydrick had a demonic, supernatural power.

I told Rob that I had read an article about Hydrick, but that I suspected that Hydrick was using various kinds of trickery to convince people of his powers. I reassured him that supernatural or superhuman powers were not in operation here, just trickery.

Rob didn't believe me.

This was not unusual. Most people relinquish their belief in the supernatural—either positive or negative—with difficulty. Age, education, wealth, social status and gullibility are not factors. One demonstration in my college presentation "Fraud and the Supernatural" points this out.

I ask a randomly selected student to think of the name of a deceased friend. There is no advance work done prior to the actual demonstration, and the participant is not a shill (not in on the act). But while the participant is concentrating on their deceased friend, I suddenly reveal the name of the person they are thinking of *and* (with a high degree of accuracy) their former relationship. Emotionally, it is jarring, but it is pulled off by trickery and not psychic powers.

Then I ask, "How many of you here [in the audience] think I have used some kind of a psychic or supernatural mind power? Raise your hands, please." Even though the audience knows of my expertise as a magician, over sixty per cent will raise their hand. This percentage of response is true regardless of the group I am in front of. Even such diverse professional groups as corporate executives and pastors of churches will give a fifty to sixty percent positive response.

Why? Because when people see a demonstration of alleged psychic or supernatural power for which they have no explanation *and* which has been presented in a *context as if it is a real power,* most people conclude that there isn't any natural explanation. My experience is that a person must *actually see* what, where and how trickery has been done before they will be convinced otherwise.

This is even true for those who are theologically trained. The reason, I believe, is that at many theological seminaries there is little or no teaching on the many types of phenomena and trickery which only appear to be supernatural.

I was a bit surprised when Rob continued to seek my help concerning his brother because I knew he didn't believe my initial explanation.

Held in the Snare
When I field calls of this kind, I try to keep an open mind. I don't usually prejudge a case before it is examined, due to an outside chance that it might be the real McCoy. The reason I'd come to a rather quick evaluation of Hydrick, though, was because of the specific demonstrations reported in the AP release. They smacked of magician's tricks.

Rob's first concern, and mine, was for the welfare of his brother, Mike, who had been released from the hospital and had returned to Salt Lake, where Hydrick had his martial arts studio. I asked if Mike was open to professional counseling by a psychologist or psychiatrist, and Rob said that he was not. After extricating someone from this kind of situation, professional counseling is often needed to repair emotional or psychological damage. I hoped Mike would consider this option after he was convinced that Hydrick did not have powers.

At Rob's urging I agreed to fly to Salt Lake where I could personally witness Hydrick's demonstrations and talk to Mike.

A few days later, I called Mike and expressed his brother's concern for his personal well-being. Not wanting to put Mike on the defensive, I carefully asked him what it was that he thought Hydrick was doing. He described numerous demonstrations, which to a magician would ring of trickery. The most impressive demonstration, not describe in the newspaper account, was Hydrick's ability to cause a borrowed dollar bill to rotate at will on the head of a pin, while under an inverted fish tank.

Hydrick had told Mike that he had refined his martial arts ability and mental prowess to the point where he could make objects move, read minds and do a number of other paranormal feats. Mike also added that two men—Chris Corey, a popular disc jockey in Salt Lake, and Mike George, a local promoter—wanted to book Hydrick on the night club circuit.

As our conversation wound down, I told Mike how I believed Hydrick fooled the AP reporter and others. I took great care not to focus attention on the fact that Mike was fooled, and thereby put him on the defensive. I spoke only of how "others" might have been deceived. It is important in this kind of a situation when a person's core beliefs are challenged, that the one being duped does not feel threatened by the logical explanation. An air of mutual exploration must be created.

"Look, how about if I fly up and take a look at what Hydrick is doing firsthand," I suggested. "If he has real powers, I'll be the first to admit it, and if he doesn't, neither you or I want him influencing others—especially not the kids in his studio." Mike seemed satisfied.

Then I asked Mike if he thought my assumption was correct that Hydrick did not possess any paranormal powers. His response was a definitive no. He was willing to investigate further, but he was personally still convinced. I asked him to keep our conversation confidential. He agreed, although I knew there was a high risk that he might tell Hydrick in an effort to protect and warn him.

The Public's Response
A few weeks earlier Hydrick had appeared on the now defunct television show "That's Incredible," an amalgam of bizarre and unusual stories and live guests. His appearance had been a direct result of the AP wire story.[1]

On national television, Hydrick presented several demonstrations, including a bravado presentation of his moving pencil stunt. Here, he caused a pencil balanced on the edge of a table to seemingly move and rotate at will. One of the hosts, John Davidson, a well-known singer, exclaimed, "I can hear you blowing on the pencil!"

With a look of defiance, Hydrick turned his head away from the pencil, concentrated and the pencil still turned. He glared at Davidson and with theatrical aplomb, triumphantly walked off the set. As a result of his appearance, Hydrick received hundreds of letters from people of all walks of life inquiring how they too could develop the same powers. What follows are some excerpts.

Hi! I live in Pomona, California. From what I've seen of you on TV, you have a lot of amazing abilities, and I would like to learn these abilities as I think it would help me grow spiritually, mentally, and physically. This is a chance of a lifetime and I would give anything to be able to become one of your students.—*Teenager*

If you do psychic healings for individuals, would it be possible for me to seek your help in curing headaches? No physician or medicine man has thus far been able to do so. My sister and I are very active seniors and wish to continue our activities in touring the back country, but these headaches have made it most difficult for us to do so.— *Senior citizen*

You've given me the first real hope I've had in months. I had tried to pay people to bring my lover back to me (a psychic, two spiritualists, and a white witch), all to no avail. Each one promised to bring him back within a few days, but after they had gotten several hundred dollars from me, they tell me it will take a lot more money which I don't have.— *Widow*

Have you read any of L. Ron Hubbard's books such as *Science of Survival* or *Dianetics—the Modern Science of Mental Health* (a current best seller)? We think you'll be able to understand yourself and others a lot better if you check out Dianetics/Scientology. . . . We think you'll find Scientology a very interesting subject—maybe even too interesting.— *Your friends at the Church of Scientology*

There were also a significant number of letters from articulate and seemingly sophisticated professionals ranging from doctors, flight attendants, attorneys, teachers and business people. This is not surprising as every formal and informal poll indicates that over sixty per cent of the population in the U.S. believe that ESP and psychic powers do exist and can be developed. Even from the scientific community, we often hear statements such as, "Human beings use only ten per cent of the capacity of their brain," and "No one really knows what untapped powers we possess." These speculations fuel the expectation that one day we will discover human powers that transcend the five senses. Here are some other examples of letters of this genre.

I am currently doing some research on the brain, nervous system and energy patterns of the human body and would very much like to discuss [this with you].—*Doctor*

I am aware of the Tibet influence on you and hope to share some avenues of my own growth in a meeting with you. If there is an interest, I look forward to your reply.—*Administrator of a mental health clinic*

I appreciated your coming to talk to my humanities class. In so many ways you are another Siddhartha. Like everyone else, I was disbelieving when I heard that you could move pencils and plants and turn pages through some unusual power. What can I say? Your abilities are astounding. Your demonstration left no doubt as to the authenticity of your power. . . . The students have written notes to you. . . . I'm sure you'll be able to tell how much they appreciated and enjoyed your presentation.—*High school teacher*

We look forward to the possibility of your coming to [our high school] for a clinic geared toward athletes. As I stated when we talked, I'm a high school swim coach and was the 1977 and 1979 State Coach of the Year [for my state]. I believe, as I'm sure you do, that whatever the mind can conceive and believe the body can achieve.—*Swim coach*

I have seen people of every walk of life make similar observations about someone they thought had powers. The remarks are almost always the same because the potential of real mind powers hits a universal chord: *the desire to control our own destinies.*

Scientific Support

Then on February 26 and later on March 2 and 5, Hydrick's credibility was further bolstered from testing done by a former assistant professor of electrical engineering, Dr. Mark Hagmann, at the University of Utah in Salt Lake City. Excerpts from his report clearly indicate that he thought Hydrick's demonstrations were genuine.

This report concerns a series of tests made in an attempt to understand the nature of the phenomena which Mr. Hydrick has demonstrated. The genuineness of such phenomena was demonstrated to my satisfaction in the testing reported earlier. Mr. Hydrick has described a "jiggling" of atoms which he sees in the objects that he moves and these tests were made to determine if such sub-microscopic motion would alter the electrical resistance of matter in the solid state.

On March 2, 1981 a 20-volt zener diode was back-biased at approximately 20 volts so that tunneling was the principal means of electrical conduction. Mr. Hydrick was told to "jiggle the particles within the diode" to see if he could increase their activity. In this and in all other tests described in this report, Mr. Hydrick did not touch the diode or other equipment. Over a period of about ten minutes a slow upward drift in electrical current was observed. In order to determine whether the drift was due to Mr. Hydrick or to malfunction of the equipment, James was told to relax and the current drifted back most of the way to the original value. Then he was told that he should apply his force suddenly at the end of a one-two-three count. On repeated counts, a ten per cent increase in current was observed followed by decay to the original value of measured electrical current. Timing of the increase in current was synchronized with the one-two-three count. Mr. Hydrick had his hands down away from the equipment during these tests.

This report was a real triumph for Hydrick as it provided credibility from the scientific community although Dr. Hagmann stated later in the report: "It would also be good to bring in one or more professional magicians who could describe how they would attempt to fake the observed phenomena and they could look for evidence that such procedures were in use."

When I met with Dr. Hagmann in his Salt Lake office, he went on to say, "Unfortunately 99 percent of what you get [with Hydrick] is fantasy. And I have to put up with it and just ignore it. Some of what he does is perhaps sleight of hand—parlor tricks . . . but there are a few things that I certainly have no way of explaining."

Good Will from a Concerned Family

Others from the Salt Lake Community not only liked Hydrick, but they took him into their home after he was paroled to Utah. They wanted to help him get a fresh start after his release from prison. One couple, whom we will call Alex and Lisa, was the hallmark of a clean-living all-American family.

Alex, an ex-marine, is a corporate attorney in Salt Lake and Lisa, of German extraction, exhibited good instincts and judgment of character. Together with their three kids, they typify a solid community-oriented family. I asked them why they took a chance on Hydrick.

"Well," Alex began, "we first met James at the end of May in 1980. He was working as a maintenance man in the athletic club that we visit and he used to do tricks for everybody."

"Like?" I queried.

"A favorite was a string trick where he tied the string in a knot and cut it and then put it in his mouth, claiming to put the molecules of the cut ends back together. Then he'd take it out of his mouth and the string would be in one piece again."

"Did you believe him?" I asked.

"No, that was the one thing that I didn't believe. I came back to my office the first time I saw it and spent about four hours with an engineer here till we figured it out," Alex said, laughing out loud.

"What about the pencils and the different objects he could move? What did you think of that?" I asked.

"Now that was believable to us, particularly when he would take our youngest boy's hand and use it to move the pencil."

"He aimed your son's hand at the pencil?" I probed.

"Right. We finally persuaded him to quit doing the string trick, because, we told him, if he really had the power to move the pencil, and then he threw in these other magicians' tricks, people would feel that the whole thing was a trick. And he wouldn't be believable. He'd lose all credibility," Alex concluded.

"What was the response of other people when they saw him make objects move?" I asked.

"Almost everybody was immediately impressed," said Alex, "particularly people who are positively oriented and believe that we're only using a fraction of our minds' power."

"I think that everybody has a certain amount of psychic power," joined in Lisa.

"Yeah, I think Lisa has some psychic power herself," said Alex. "Our phone rings a lot because we have two teenagers. But a lot of times when I call home, Lisa will pick up the phone and say, 'Hello, Alex. I knew you were calling.' It just seems that there's got to be more to it than just chance."

Alex is right: there is more to it than just chance, but it's not psychic. My wife, Sandy, does the same thing with our friend, Bill Noble. And she is correct almost one hundred per cent of the time. But she will tell you that it has to do with the number of times that he calls, his work schedule, whether she knows that he is wrestling with something and he needs counsel, and other factors.

One night we had Bill and a female friend of ours over for dinner to make a low-key introduction. About three minutes after our guests left, the phone rang. Before I picked up the phone, Sandy said, "Tell

Bill it's okay. We know that she isn't his type."

I picked up the receiver and before the caller identified himself, I said, "Bill, Sandy told me to tell you it's okay. We know that Janet isn't for you."

The only sound I heard from the receiver was Bill's stammering. He was floored. I let him off the hook when I explained that Sandy knew he had a phone in his car and he was probably calling to be polite about not being interested in Janet.

"But Sandy knows when I'm calling every stinking time!" he insisted. "I know, she's really a psychic, and you're hiding her from the world!"

Sandy and I have a good laugh whenever she intimidates him with her "psychic powers." But if one hasn't really thought something like this through, it can appear to be real, as it did to Alex and Lisa.

Lisa told me, however, that Hydrick's apparent psychic abilities didn't influence their decision to take him in to their home. They simply wanted to help him overcome the childhood abuse he had suffered by living with a stable family. They were sure that his childhood had contributed to his criminal record, which Hydrick had forthrightly shared with them.

Alex added, "We're basically positive people, and we felt that he really wanted to make a change. So his past didn't really bother us that much."

Lisa and Alex's concern for Hydrick was typical of how most people regarded him: local law enforcement officials, crime prevention officers when Hydrick was a teen-ager, foster parents and the man on the street. A blend of intrigue about his "powers" and a sense of caring about a kid who had been abused drew people to him.

Hydrick's personality was complex, loving one moment and suspicious the next, wanting to be a part of the world and then intensely desiring to escape.

"His overwhelming desire at the time," Alex said, "was to just leave and go out in the mountains and not have anything to do with people anymore. He didn't trust people, he didn't like people. He wanted to be in the mountains by himself. He had a never-ending fear of being alone. . . . Anything that would happen, he would immediately see it as directed at him personally."

Hydrick presented an intense challenge to anyone who took the time to get to know him. He challenged what they believed about the workings of the mind and how a maligned person is to function in society. I was not excluded.

Mike in Desperate Straits

Alex had been one of those staying with Hydrick and Mike at the Beverly Wilshire Hotel in Los Angeles when Mike had his emotional breakdown. He had witnessed it firsthand.

"One night Mike started talking about devil possession and different experiences that he'd had," said Alex. "You know . . . there was some numerology and various other strange things that had happened to him in the past. He thought they were all supernatural, and he believed that James was connected to them all.

"And then," Alex continued hesitantly, "Mike just lost contact with reality . . . for several days. No one could get him out of the hotel. . . . He wouldn't eat; he wouldn't get dressed. Finally, they just had to take him to the psychiatric clinic at the UCLA hospital."

Hydrick's "powers" attracted a diverse group of believers and supporters. Some were emotionally and mentally balanced. Others weren't. And the continued media exposure had broadened and strengthened his influence. It was hard to tell whether Hydrick posed a manipulative threat to those around him, or whether Mike's problems were primarily independent of Hydrick, or a little of both.

I was convinced, though, that this was something worth capturing on tape—something that could benefit others. The question was how to do it and at the same time help Mike.

Chapter 7

Hydrick's Background

ALTHOUGH I HAD A LOT OF EXPERIENCE EXPOSING VARIOUS TYPES OF FAKERY, dating back to my college days at Tulane University in New Orleans, I had never filmed an actual case.

In 1979 and 1980 a couple of different news shows asked me about participating in an exposé, but I declined for fear of losing control of the investigative process. Most news broadcasts tend to sensationalize this kind of a story, not treating it seriously nor showing its potential for wreaking havoc.

Lacking even elementary production experience, I called a producer in Dallas and asked him to accompany me to Salt Lake. If I could convince Hydrick to let me tape him, I would then have a producer on line with a feel for the production logistics.

First Contact
I contacted Hydrick the first week of February. I briefly told Hydrick in
a long distance phone call that I wanted to meet him because I was
considering producing a program on those who claim to have psychic
powers. Preoccupied at the time, he tentatively agreed, referring me to
his "agent," Mike George.

George was working in tandem with Chris Corey, one of Salt Lake's
top DJs, to promote their new talent. I was aloofly informed that James
was to appear on Johnny Carson's "Tonight Show." (This never materialized.) But George did agree to consider an "offer" after I witnessed
Hydrick's powers with my own eyes. He said he would get back with
me on a date when I could fly up.

"He's really hot right now and everybody wants him. Just be patient,"
he closed.

In subsequent calls, George continued to put me off. The delay made
me anxious. It only increased the chances that Mike might talk to Hydrick or that Mike could have another breakdown.

As I feared, something did happen that severely complicated my attempts.

Almost Spooked
On February 24 Hydrick appeared on another national television show,
"That's My Line," which featured guests with unusual occupations. It was
on this show that he was challenged by James "The Amazing" Randi,
a magician with a reputation for exposing various types of fakers. Randi
has had a standing $10,000 offer to anyone who can demonstrate a bona
fide psychic or supernatural feat. To date, no one has ever claimed his
check.

During the broadcast, Hydrick was to demonstrate his powers by
turning the pages of a telephone book without touching them. Hydrick
had impressively presented this demonstration on a number of pro-

grams. What he didn't know was that Randi would appear on the show with him.

Although short in stature, the peppery bearded magician stood tall in his challenge to Hydrick. He insisted on one test. Hydrick had to turn the pages in his phone book demonstration with the book surrounded by Styrofoam "peanuts"—the kind used in packing cases. If Hydrick tried to blow on the pages to make them turn, which was Randi's theory, the Styrofoam peanuts scattered on the table top would also move.

For an hour and a half a frustrated Hydrick tried without success. Only a few minutes of his attempts actually aired. Defeated, the response from the viewing audience was not what one would expect. Several hundred letters were received by the producers of the show. Only one was pro-Randi. The rest castigated Randi for the manner in which he tried to

Hydrick turns pages in a telephone book without touching them.

expose Hydrick and expressed sympathy for Hydrick.

One reason for this response, some speculate, is Randi's sometimes caustic nature. A mutual friend, Dr. Ray Hyman, points out that Randi can appear to be one who is out to get the psychic, rather than one who wants to expose someone in response to his compassion for the victim.

But a more important factor is that many people *want to believe* that these kinds of mind powers do exist. The net effect was that Hydrick's followers became more ardent in their belief in Hydrick and his ability to teach them how to have the same powers.

After this confrontation, Hydrick, however, became virtually inaccessible to outsiders. As a result, my seeing him became almost impossible. The effect of his maligned past kicked into high gear.

Hydrick's Early Years

James Allen Hydrick was born on February 28, 1959, in Passaic, New Jersey, to Billy Louie and Bertha (Lois) Dickens Hydrick. Reports I later obtained with Hydrick's permission from various government agencies stated that Lois was an alcoholic and deserted James and his brother and sister when James was only three years old.

I hired Hugh Aynesworth, a seasoned investigative journalist with several Pulitzer Prize nominations, to assist me. Together we interviewed Lois at nine in the morning in her trailer home just off Tobacco Road in Augusta, Georgia. Chickens flapped noisily in the barren back yard.

A thirty-seven-year-old house painter, she looked much older draped in her green terry-cloth housecoat. As she sipped from her can of Bud, she told us her story.

"Hell, when I left Billy I left him with all four young'uns," she said with vehemence. "But Billy was a wife beater. I was fifteen years old when I married him, and he was thirty. I had nothing but kids. I didn't know nothing. By the time I was twenty-one I had four kids." (One child was from Billy's first marriage.)

When asked if she ever abused James, she denied it. However, she began recalling incidents that suggested problems.

"Yeah. I tied them to the bed after they got into forty penicillin tablets, and I had to take them to the hospital and get their stomachs pumped out. So the next night, I tied them to the bed. I tied their ankles—one ankle, each kid. . . . But I ain't never tied them to the bed since," she said as if they were still living with her, eighteen years later.

She recalled another incident when James was three years old and "messed his bed."

"I woke up one morning. . . . I knew it was in the cold winter-time. . . . God, I just started gagging from the smell. I put him in the bathtub, and I meant to turn on cold water, but I turned on . . . warm water, well, hot water. But I . . . I didn't scald him."

Hydrick's aunt, Bobby Jean, his father's sister, claimed she saw one incident of abuse firsthand when the transient family was staying with her in Aiken, South Carolina, a quaint southern town noted for its thoroughbred horses.

The Hydrick family lived in a run-down across-the-tracks section of town where dogs with mange whimpered down gravel roads. One of Hydrick's few toys, a rubber ball attached to a wooden paddle by a long rubber band that is sold in most dime stores, was the instrument of abuse.

"Well, at one time, when they were staying with me, James was crying in the middle of the night. And his mother got up, and she took the rick-rack paddle, the end that you hold in your hand, she took it and put it up his rectum." Each of the other children also experienced severe physical and emotional abuse, as related by the aunt and other foster parents.

Deserted by his wife, Billy was also separated from his son for two years when Hydrick was six. Billy served on a chain gang for two years after being convicted of armed robbery.

Billy reluctantly spoke with me in front of his modest rural home in Aiken, South Carolina, while Mary, his second wife, peered through the window at us. Mary's teen-age kids observed us as they leaned against Billy's red pickup.

A former alcoholic, he recalled in a slow southern drawl his earliest memories of James.

"Well, when I was working them honky-tonks and couldn't get no-body to stay with him, I kept him in the car outside the joint a lot of times. He'd sleep right there in the back of my station wagon." He kept his voice low, perhaps not wanting his other kids to hear.

Billy's upbringing mirrored James's in many respects. "My father was in the Army for thirty years, and . . . well, I was three months old when [my parents] separated."

"Who did you live with after that?" I asked.

"One time it was a foster home."

"And who did you grow up with as a teen-ager?"

"Just a wild bunch," replied Billy, staring at his shoe tops.

Everyone I interviewed who knew the family recollected that all three of Billy and Lois's kids had been abused.

State Reports

The state records show that Hydrick and his brother and sister were shuffled around to various foster homes and state agencies, until Hy-drick was sent by his father—at the age of nine—to Whitten Center, an institution for the mentally retarded in South Carolina. He was admitted even though he was *not* mentally retarded. What follows is drawn from various reports that further reveal his early life.

☐ In the summer of 1963 James, age 4, "was accepted at Southern Christian Home in Atlanta, Ga. [where he stayed] until the spring of 1965. . . . We do not know why the home dismissed him, except that he was a behavior problem from the beginning. . . ."

He was "then placed in Tabernacle Baptist Children's Home in Greenville, S.C., until June 1966 when they asked to have him re-moved because of a disciplinary problem. . . .

"He has since been in five foster homes. . . .

"He is repeating the first grade. . . . His attention span is short. . . . He does not accept authority. . . . He was not able to play with other children because he would play too rough and eventually hurt them, so he could gain power. This was done intentionally and did not have to be prompted. . . . His father and stepmother are not capable of loving the child." (Aiken County Welfare Department, 5/29/67).

☐ "The final possibility . . . would be placement at Whitten Center. We pointed out that the boy is not retarded, but there is no question that he is in acute need of special education since he is unable to learn in a regular class situation with the problem of dyslexia" (State Progress Report, 1/30/69).

☐ "James contends that he is not retarded. He reports: 'Everyone says I don't need to be here.' James appears to associate retardation with 'acting crazy.' . . . 'I've got good sense,' he said. . . . There is a measure of basic truth in his beliefs regarding this issue. . . . Data yields a mental age of eleven years and eight months. . . . He has no current medical problems, but uses tranquilizing medication" (Whitten Center, 4/5/74).

The next two years consisted of more of the same—life in institutions and ineffective parental and foster care.

On December 9, 1977, when Hydrick was eighteen, he hitchhiked to Los Angeles to live with some other youths. According to the police, he was arrested and charged for kidnapping and robbery.

Transcripts state that Hydrick and four companions abducted two homosexuals in the Beverly Hills area of California. The victims testified that they were pulled into a van and had their clothes cut off with a long knife. Then they were beaten and robbed. One was forced to perform a sex act on one of the abductors before both victims were thrown from the moving van. Hydrick denied any involvement in the sexual assault.

Two years passed while Hydrick was held in the Los Angeles County Jail. Finally, after pleading guilty to the kidnapping and robbery charges, he was sentenced on January 9, 1979, and received a fifteen-year sentence which was reduced to three years—two of which he had already served—plus one year probation.

"Psychic" Origins

It was while he was in the Los Angeles County Jail that Hydrick began developing his "psychic" abilities and became fascinated with the cultic writings of Muharem Kurbegovic. (Kurbegovic, dubbed the "Alphabet Bomber," was convicted of planting a bomb in a locker at the Los Angeles International Airport on August 6, 1975. It exploded killing three persons and injuring thirty-six others.)

To pass the time in jail, Hydrick, possessing an impressive six-foot-one-inch physique, also resumed a freelance study of the martial arts he had started as a youth in Aiken. Chester Cromwell, one of the few positive, foster-parent role models Hydrick had, said Hydrick often dreamed of being the new "Bruce Lee," the star of many "B" quality martial arts films.

Hydrick told me how he extricated himself from a threat by the leader of a black gang while in jail. Cornered, Hydrick claims he knocked out the gang leader with one punch. An officer at the Los Angeles County Jail, Peggy Wiggenhorn, confirmed the altercation and that the gang member was extremely dangerous. She stated that remaining in the facility could have been life-threatening to Hydrick.

At the urging of Brother Gerald Chumik, a priest who befriended Hydrick, Hydrick was paroled to Salt Lake City in the early spring of 1980, in part for his protection and also for good behavior. In May of 1980, Hydrick met Alex and Lisa and later befriended Mike.

With a combination of tall tales, "psychic" demonstrations and extraordinary physical prowess, Hydrick quickly gained a following in Salt Lake, where he worked out at a local gym and had a job as a janitor. His recent parole didn't seem to scare people off or make them leery.

The local press picked up on Hydrick—a good story about a hard-luck kid with extraordinary mind powers. On November 14, 1980, Lee Benson, a sports writer for the *Deseret News,* after cataloging a list of Hydrick's powers, wrote: "I was converted enough to write this article. If what he's done and what he does isn't on the level . . . then he's put the fakeout on an honest-to-goodness American sportswriter. And that's not easy. Everybody knows sports writers may be the most skeptical of our modern race."

The Associated Press story I read first appeared in the *Deseret News* on December 11, 1980. Producers for "That's Incredible," prompted by the article and a viewing of a local television show featuring Hydrick, taped Hydrick in mid-December and aired the program on December 29, 1980. Barely literate, Hydrick was for the first time in his life getting recognition.

When Randi on "That's My Line" attempted to expose Hydrick two months later, Hydrick's meteoric recognition was threatened. He trusted no one. Only after numerous calls and tediously absorbing Hydrick's anxiety was I able to arrange a date to meet with him—March 17, 1981.

Chapter 8

The First Meeting with Hydrick

ACOUPLE OF DAYS BEFORE FLYING TO SALT LAKE, I CALLED MIKE MARTIN TO find out how he was doing. He said that he would not be in Salt Lake when I arrived. He sounded shaky but more stable than the last time I spoke with him. I maintained regular phone contact to monitor his condition and hopefully gain his trust. I feared that his fierce loyalty to Hydrick might win out over reason. His absence from Salt Lake when I was due to arrive was actually an asset as the focus of attention on this first trip needed to be on Hydrick.

Accompanied by a freelance producer, I flew to Salt Lake where we were greeted at the airport by Rose Jackson. Rose and her husband Phil had taken over Alex and Lisa's role, letting Hydrick live with them after

Lisa and Alex realized Hydrick was more than they could handle. Alex told me that if they had had professional counsel in working with him, they might have been able to continue to carry the torch, but his erratic behavior was too much for their family of five.

Suggestive Powers

Rose's two sons were enrolled in Hydrick's martial arts classes. Unlike Alex and Lisa, Rose and her family seemed naive and susceptible to Hydrick's charisma. Rose excitedly spoke of Hydrick's appearance on "That's Incredible" and hoped the show we were working on would be as adventuresome. On the way to the studio, Rose related some of her experiences with Hydrick's powers.

"One time he had me move a pencil, and when he touched me I felt a kind of tingling . . . like a shot of electricity going through me."

An account of this kind is not uncommon. Those who come in physical contact with alleged psychics moving objects or those who claim that they can transfer psychic energy to heal someone will often tell of an electric jolt or shock. The experience is not real, but imagined. This does not mean that a person is unbalanced, rather just susceptible to suggestion.

For the same demonstration I explained earlier, I once asked a woman about the same age as Rose to write down the name of a deceased acquaintance on a small slip of paper. After the name of the deceased was revealed, I instructed the participant to hold the folded slip in her outstretched hand.

"I want you to concentrate on the name and in a moment or two you will begin to feel heat in your hand and the slip will get hot," I suggested intently.

Within a few seconds she acknowledged that it was indeed getting hot, and a transparent look of fright flashed across her face. I then explained to her and the audience how suggestion—not the paper—made her hand feel hot.

There is a trick, however, where one holds a crumpled piece of foil in one's hand and it really does get hot. The modus operandi is a simple one. A highly toxic chemical solution is secretly applied to the foil as it is given to the participant. He or she is then instructed to close the foil into a ball and to think "heat." After a few seconds the chemical begins to react with the foil and it does get hot. When the participant drops the foil because of the increased temperature, it cools on its descent to the floor. The "psychic" then picks it up without discomfort, gives it back to the participant and the trick is once again repeated.

This second method when *combined* with the first method, which relies upon suggestion, is very convincing. To the uninitiated, it becomes impossible for one to know what to believe. Was it trickery? Was it suggestion? The clever interweaving of *physical trickery* (in this example the use of a chemical) with more natural principles (like suggestion) makes it possible to create the illusion that one is a "gifted" individual. Rose was convinced that Hydrick was gifted because of her intense personal experience.

Hydrick's Studio

We arrived in the early afternoon at Hydrick's studio. It was located in a middle-to-lower income section of Salt Lake. The front window of the old corrugated-steel-roofed building sported a dragon and other symbols one expects to see on a martial arts storefront. Inside on the gym's hardwood floor, students, ranging in age from six to fifty, were stretching and practicing different blocks and punches. Hydrick's promoter, Mike George (not Mike Martin), greeted us.

He ushered us upstairs to Hydrick's one-bedroom living quarters overlooking the gym floor. The room was dimly lit and decorated with martial arts posters and weapons, including a set of brass knuckles that had several razor sharp edges. My producer recoiled when he eyed the weapons. He was visibly uncomfortable. We were told that the reason we were to meet Hydrick here was that it was where he felt most at ease when "trying to release his focused energies."

After a few minutes of George's chatter, Hydrick entered the room dressed in a red karate-gi. At a quick glance he *did* look like the poster of Bruce Lee hanging on his wall. Hydrick's moustache and hair were dyed black to mirror Lee.

We shook hands. His grip was tentative, and he was discomposed on the heels of the Randi confrontation. He looked us over carefully as we engaged in small talk about his studio. He relaxed a little when I told him that I had heard about the testing by Dr. Hagmann. Excitedly, Hydrick embarked on a retelling of the validation of his powers.

He claimed it all began when he met Master Wu at Loch and Dam on the Savannah River outside Augusta, Georgia, just across the state line from Aiken. Loch and Dam is exactly what the name implies—a small lake off the Savannah created by a small dam. There, in the early morning, with the mist rising off the water and distorting the moss-laden trees along the bank, he met an old Chinese man who became his mentor and taught him how to develop his extraordinary powers.

"I had never seen a Chinese man before . . . and there's this little ol' Chinese man, I guess, about five-foot-four. . . . He had a strange lookin' hat and he had a cane. . . . And he just stood there motioning to me to come.

"His English wasn't that good, but it was good enough to understand, and he would say, 'To you in my eyes I see a new, a strange animal in a new land.' And he would talk . . . in riddles. Like he would say, 'Come with me and teach you, I will, of this jungle.' [Or,] 'I see through your heart pain and sorrow.'

"I began then my training in martial arts and I began in his mental training. He would put his hands all over my head, and it would numb my whole body," Hydrick said, reminiscent of the hero from "Kung Fu," a television show from the seventies. The series followed the exploits of a young man without family roots who traveled the old west. He protected himself and others with martial arts skills so highly developed that they appeared to be superhuman.

Hydrick also explained how he unbalanced opponents by letting out a special yell, "Thdok wuuu."

"It disturbs the body," he explained, "therefore the person is unbalanced."

Hydrick's stories were often bits of truth from his past, mystically told stories that made it easier for him to accept his background and be accepted by others. In subsequent interviews he admitted that there was no Master Wu, Hydrick's imaginary mentor created while locked in a closet for long periods of time as punishment when he was a young boy. In the closet he would pretend that he could travel to foreign countries where he was welcomed.

He also told how he was used as alligator bait after he was sold into child slavery by his father. The story, a fabrication, was constructed, "Because if I made up stories worse than what actually happened, then I wouldn't have to remember what really happened to me," Hydrick later admitted.

Then suddenly, without prompting, he lashed out at the efforts of James Randi to debunk him. To Hydrick, Randi was a monstrous threat, threatening his newfound acceptance into society as well as his own self-acceptance. He said, "Randi is filled with hatred."

Demonstrations

Changing the subject to divert his seething anger toward Randi, I told him that I was anxious to see a demonstration of his abilities. His tricks were the safest part of his person to untangle. Although restless, he calmed down and went to work.

To begin with, he showed me feats of physical prowess. Starting with a speed test, he placed a credit card on the table. We then each positioned one hand next to the credit card.

"Any time you want, try and cover the credit card as quickly as you can. But I'll beat you," he instructed. "Master Wu taught me this so I could sneak up on a bird and catch it with my bare hand."

I went along with him. The secret to this school boy's stunt is one of simply anticipating when your opponent will make his move. His next demonstration, though, caught me off guard.

I have read thousands of books and trade publications on sleight-of-hand tricks but have never heard of a stunt as shrewdly managed as Hydrick's "attack" trick. It's one thing to invent a trick if you are properly trained and well read, but it's another to invent new tricks with nothing behind you but your own instinct of what will fool others. If a test could measure one's cleverness, I suspect Hydrick would score in the top percentile.

He instructed me to take my pulse. Then, feeding off his martial arts aura, he said, "The reason I can fight blindfolded is because, before a punch is thrown, the heart skips, and I can tell it."

He then told me that he would "listen" to my heart beat and tap his two fingers together until I told him that he was tapping in rhythm to my pulse. When I nodded that he was tapping his fingers in time with my pulse, he said, "Now any time you want, just think 'attack.' And because I can hear your heart beat, I will hear it skip, and I'll tell you when you thought 'attack.' "

This was new to me. Earlier I had viewed footage of Hydrick blocking slow punches while he was blindfolded. The secret is beguilingly simple. He merely peeked down the bridge of his nose. When he detected any kind of movement in the person's body standing opposite from him, he would swing his arm up to block the punch. It was an old trick. But for this new twist, I didn't have a clue what to expect.

About ten seconds later I thought "attack," and the moment I did, Hydrick said, "Now!"

I was amazed.

"And I have no wires hooked up to me so I can hear your heart beat," he emphasized. By my reaction, he knew that he had won me over.

The Secret

If I was fooled, it was easy to see how anyone who lacked my training might be overwhelmed by this seemingly impromptu portrayal of extrasensory perception. There were no props and nothing to physically manipulate. Even if a person didn't believe that Hydrick was a psychic, they would believe that he had *something* that they didn't.

Quickly assessing the principles Hydrick might harness, I guessed that he was using one of the principles of cold reading, micro-expressions—in this case minute movement of facial features that told him when someone was thinking "attack." My assessment was correct.

I speculated that when I thought "attack," my face or body must have moved almost imperceptibly. The tapping of his fingers and my feeling my pulse were merely to get me to register a fixed expression on my face, similar to one staring at one's palm or Tarot Cards during a reading. Then, when I thought "attack," my intense gaze would flicker just enough for Hydrick to pick it up. Also, a cursory perception of the subject's personality could help one anticipate *when* a particular person might think "attack."

To test my theory, I determined only to think "attack" *after* I deliberately twitched my right eyebrow. My hunch was correct. Hydrick missed on his next attempt, and he was surprised. To avoid putting put him on the defensive, I let him correctly guess on his third attempt, and I dismissed his failure by blaming it on my lack of concentration and intensity.

I was impressed by Hydrick's mastery of natural principles which could easily give the appearance, even to skeptics, of real powers. The best tricks have the feeling of being presented on the spur of the moment without props or special set-ups.

The believability of the "attack" trick was etched in my producer's face. He asked me, when we were alone for a few minutes, "Did he really know?" When I replied, "Yes," I thought I would have to scrape him off the floor. I didn't tell him *how* Hydrick knew until later. I wanted to see how he reacted and handled the encounter. (To my dismay, he became increasingly apprehensive. When we got back to Dallas he pulled out: he was afraid, as were most producers I contacted, of Hydrick. Filming Hydrick was a long way from producing commercials or an industrial film with a carefully planned script.)

Hydrick then took us downstairs to the gym, where he showed off his very impressive one-thumb pushup. I have been around many professional athletes, and none have been able to duplicate this test of strength. Then, grinning like a young boy on a little league field looking for his father's approval, he demonstrated how high he could jump. He leaped and kicked the net of the basketball goal, nine feet off the ground. Then with mounting enthusiasm he demonstrated a number of blocks, moves and punches he said that he originated. Even though they weren't original, as he claimed, I was literally taken back by his one-inch punch.

He had me stand in front of him holding a flat pad that was one-inch thick and the size of a catcher's mitt. The pad was held between my two

Hydrick demonstrates his one-thumb pushup.

hands against my chest to help absorb the blow. He held his fist out only one inch from my chest. Without recoiling, he then unleashed a blow that sent me reeling backward several feet, the force of the blow nearly knocking the wind out of me.

I later asked a friend of mine, Keith Yates—a sixth-degree black belt in *Tae Kwon Do,* the Korean form of Karate—about this stunt and the authenticity of Hydrick's martial arts skills. Keith said, "He certainly is gifted athletically, but he is not an expert. He knows just enough, however, to give the impression that he is. The one-inch punch can be duplicated by others, but perhaps not with the same amount of force, which is what makes it look so effective."

Keith also said that Hydrick was not the first to combine Karate with claims of mental powers, although no one had attained the same degree of notoriety as Hydrick. Keith does not teach Eastern mystical concepts in his classes. His classes are strictly for sport and self-defense.

"If you can convincingly demonstrate that you are an expert in the martial arts, it would be a simple thing to convince your students that you have developed mind powers because of a study of Eastern philosophy. One gives credibility to the other," he points out.

Mind over Matter?

We then retreated upstairs again to Hydrick's one-bedroom efficiency. The air was infused with incense and Oriental strains of music.

We sat on a rug which covered the cracked tile floor. In front of me was a small square coffee table. Handing me some pencils, he asked me to examine them to be sure that they were just ordinary pencils. "Or I'll use one of yours," he offered. I was now going to see the famous rotating pencil that he presented on "That's Incredible." What I didn't expect, though I should have, was that it looked even more convincing in person than on television. Whenever someone sees me do a trick in person that they have seen on television, the response is the same: "It looked good on TV, but I never thought it would look this good with people all around you."

Hydrick kneeled at one side of the table, holding one of the pencils that I had examined. Carefully he balanced the pencil on the edge so that half of it hung over the edge. The part over the table was slightly raised like a teeter-totter.

Concentrating intensely, Hydrick glared at the pencil and then slowly moved his hand back and forth a few inches from the tip that extended over the table's edge, as if he were trying to transmit energy from his finger tips. After a minute of failing to cause the pencil to turn, theatrically embellished with a furrowed brow and pursed lips, the pencil tip rotated—first toward him and then a moment later, away from him.

Triumphantly, Hydrick stopped and said, "When I was on 'That's Incredible,' John Davidson said I was blowin'. No way. So I turned my head, and it still moved. Did he look dumb!"

Note how the end of the pencil over the table is raised slightly enabling the pencil to turn freely when hit by a puff of air.

Hydrick then turned away from the pencil, *and while his head was turned,* it again rotated.

I suspected the modus operandi still involved gentle puffs of air that Hydrick exhaled despite his protestations, but I wasn't completely sure until I returned to Dallas where I could test my theory.

There is an old trick that was in the first magic book I received as a boy, *Scarne's Magic* by John Scarne, where one places a straw on a table. It then mysteriously rolls back and forth without the use of any hidden gimmicks. The secret is simple. One merely has to exhale a gentle puff of air at *the table's surface,* and the current will carry *along the surface* to the straw causing it to roll away from the performer. Hydrick used this same principle but in a far more clever guise.

The first time Hydrick exhaled a puff at the table, his head was turned toward the table. The end of the pencil extending past the edge rotated *toward* him, as he feigned emitting energy from his finger tips. The fact that *this* end of the pencil rotated *toward* Hydrick would preclude in an onlooker's mind that Hydrick blew on the pencil. Why? Because if Hydrick blew on the extended end of the pencil, one would expect this end of the pencil to rotate *away* from Hydrick. (Hydrick later confided that it was while he was in that jail he practiced exhaling undetectable puffs of air. A powerfully developed diaphragm was the only "gimmick" he needed to perfectly execute the ruse.)

To cause the pencil tip to rotate away from him, he also used two methods. In the first method he exhaled a puff of air at the section of the pencil extending past the table's edge. For this second technique, his hands were the gimmick. Gracefully, he would move one of his slightly cupped hands away from him in such a manner as to cause a small pocket of air to hit the pencil and cause it to rotate away from him in a counterclockwise direction.

So how did he cause the extended end of the pencil to rotate toward him when his head was turned away from the table? Some experimentation provided the answer.

If the puff of air is exhaled just *before* the head is turned, there is a time lapse of a couple of seconds before the air current reaches the pencil. This creates the illusion that the head is turned *before* the pencil turns. When the movement of the pencil is combined with a mock pulling action of the hand towards the body, it looks as if the hand is transferring energy to make the pencil move.

Movement under Glass

Hydrick elusively perfected several techniques for performing each stunt. This helped rule out any explanation that might be offered. Great magicians never use obvious methods in an obvious way. One's tracks must be covered. Turning his head convinced most that he was not using air currents. But the final illusion, which took in Dr. Hagmann, was his best.

"Mike George tells me that there is a demonstration that you do with a dollar bill and a fish tank. Is that the tank he is talking about?" I asked pointing to the fish tank in the corner of the room.

"Yeah, but I don't know," he responded hesitantly.

"I would really like to see it. Please try," I prodded. He consistently eluded my first requests and would then acquiesce. Such is the stuff of a good showman and that which attracts the curious. If the "psychic" does not offer at least one or two comments such as, "I am starting to feel tired," or, "That last test has drained me quite a bit," it looks too easy and some of the believability diminishes.

Striking a more pensive mood, he asked me for a dollar bill. He folded it along its length so that it formed an inverted V. He then asked me to examine a small block of wood which had a straight pin pushed into its center. Satisfied that I did not suspect trickery, he put the block on the table and carefully balanced the folded dollar on the head of the pin, so the dollar rested like a tent. Over this he placed the fish tank. When the bill was completely still, he said, "I'll try and make the bill turn on the pin."

Inching closer to the tank with outstretched arms, he slowly moved his hands back and forth near the wall of the tank as if trying to awaken the bill. I saw no apparent way that he could control the bill. The placement of the fish tank over the bill seemed to preclude the use of air currents. But after two or three minutes of circling the tank on his knees, accompanied by hard stares, the bill began to slowly turn and completed three revolutions.

"I'll make it . . . go back the other way," he stated as if under great stress. Immediately the bill began to turn in the opposite direction. I was amazed. Hydrick was several feet away from the tank. My first reaction was that he had used some electronic device in the table to start the bill turning, but I reasoned that it *must* be something simple—consistent with his other tricks. I scrutinized every movement, simultaneously keeping my eye on George, who might be an accomplice.

After a couple of minutes, I realized that the bill only started to rotate when he was at one end of the tank. Surreptitiously, I moved toward that end of the tank.

Then I saw it—a small space, little more than a crack at one corner between the table's surface and the bottom edge of the tank. What did this mean? If Hydrick were to exhale a puff of air on the table's surface, it could carry underneath the tank's edge and hit the dollar bill setting it in motion. This was brilliant.

As I watched, he first exhaled the puff of air through his immobile lips, and then he slowly moved around the tank. The air current, taking a few seconds to reach the dollar, hit the bill *after* he was away from the corner in question. This created the illusion that he could be anywhere and the bill would still move.

The natural action of the bill when it stops turning, is to recoil and rotate in the opposite direction; thus, it will reverse its direction without additional puffs of air. This was the secret of how he could cause the bill to stop and rotate in the opposite direction even though he might be several feet from the tank! If anyone thought he was blowing on the pencils to make them turn, the bill in the fishtank would destroy that explanation.

I later came across a letter that explained how Hydrick came up with the fish tank trick, innovated after his appearance on "That's Incredible." A man who figured out the secret to the pencil trick sent a letter to the producers of the show, which was forwarded to Hydrick. The last paragraph of that letter illustrates that necessity is the mother of invention: "Why don't you have the 'telekinetic' back on your show and have him do the same feat with the balanced pencil inside a glass box!"

Moving Punching Bags

Confident that I was impressed, Hydrick took me downstairs. He gathered about twenty students, who were hanging around the gym hoping that they might be used in the special. He had them lie down in

Hydrick's students meditate under his direction and "cause the bags to start swinging."

the middle of the gym floor. They were surrounded by several punching bags and hanging ropes used during class. One of the students turned up the volume of the Oriental music ever present over the loudspeakers. For several minutes Hydrick led them through several breathing and meditation exercises.

Then he said, "I want you to concentrate and cause the bags to start swinging . . . cause them to start swinging. Cause the building to crack, to rotate . . . that's good."

Almost on cue, after a few minutes of sustained encouragement, the bags *did* begin to swing and one *could* hear the building starting to creak and groan. Again I was caught off guard. I didn't think that he could really pull it off. There were no threads attached to the bags or the ropes. I also ruled out, after careful examination, other possible explanations, such as hidden weights inside the rope or bags which could be secretly released.

The television special I finally produced on Hydrick, "Psychic Confession," did not explain how he made the bags and ropes move, even though I finally figured out the secret. It was the only one of his displays of "power" that I didn't expose. Why? Because experience dictates that when you reveal the mechanics behind every deception, people think they can no longer be fooled and adopt a false sense of security. But the fact is that we are all vulnerable to deception, regardless of what we do or don't know.

So by holding back the explanation, I left those who viewed "Psychic Confession" with the subliminal knowledge that they could still be fooled. Hydrick's students, though, were not as fortunate. If Hydrick could actually convince them that they could have the same "power," then the seeds for a cult could easily be planted.

Watching the kids and adults on the gym floor, eyes closed, slowly breathing in and out, meditating on moving bags and buildings, reminded me of the fact that Charles Manson and Jim Jones both used tricks to convince their followers that they had real powers: a simple beginning for something that ultimately destroyed human life. While I didn't perceive that Hydrick posed the same kind of threat, he did convey violent tendencies and thoughts.

With an array of martial arts equipment displayed on his twin bed, he had earlier remarked, "We have outside and inside training quarters. And what I'll do is, without my students even knowing it, I will take them downtown and have them attacked, not to where they will be hurt, but to where they can actually experience real combat." I tried to corroborate this claim with one of his students, but none would do so. If it was simply an invented story, the mere fact that he might fantasize about doing something like this made me and the local police cautious of everyone surrounding him.

Hydrick had opened his studio after Janice Schrock, a forty-five-year-old divorcee, gave him $16,000. She wanted him to realize his goal of establishing "a monastery where I can work with children and bring them up to all have this mental power." Schrock also wanted him to meet Swami Creananda, whose real name is allegedly John Donald Walters. He set up a communal-type community in northern California. She thought Hydrick could learn a lot living in this closed community. Then, in one of the never-ending twists and turns of Hydrick's life, she adopted him in April of 1981.

"I just felt that he needed a mother. And it was interesting because it was almost a compulsion. A couple of times I went to talk to him, and I would turn around and go home saying, 'This is stupid!' But one day I followed through. You know, I always wanted a son of my own," she explained.

"He was twenty-two years old," I pointed out. "Didn't you think that might be an unusual relationship, adopting somebody that old?"

"Yes," she said, "But he was interested in a monastery, and I had connections in this respect. And I thought that if he had made up his mind that that's what he wants to do, then I could help him in a lot of things."

Hydrick wanted attention and a family environment to feel secure. I don't believe he set out to form a cult, but it was increasingly apparent that a shrewd person, determined to do so, could easily manipulate him to cause that to happen without Hydrick ever perceiving the significance of what was afoot. His desire for recognition made him quick to ride the influence of anyone who could help him become more tolerable to himself and acceptable to others.

As I watched the bags hypnotically swing back and forth in his gym, I could visualize the opportunity Mike Martin had seen in Hydrick. Perhaps the talented and emotionally troubled racquetball player thought that under Hydrick's tutelage he too could develop his mental powers just enough to influence that small fast-moving black ball to move only an inch on the court—away from an opponent's racket. And the secret of how the bags moved? The stuff of an opportunist.

Around 3:00 to 3:30 in the afternoon, the old corrugated metal building would begin to heat up under the Utah sun and start to shift due to expansion. The effect—the building would creak, and the bags and ropes would begin to sway. Hydrick merely had to wait until he heard the first minute popping of the metal—which was covered by the ethereal music—and then tell his students, "Cause the building to crack, to rotate. Cause the bags to start swinging . . . swinging."

Simple? Yes. But clever enough to fool even the most skeptical.

To convince Mike Martin and others that Hydrick didn't have powers would require ironclad, videotaped proof. Nothing less would work because Hydrick was constantly inventing new methods to stifle his critics. The question was how to expose his tricks on camera without tipping him off or his following. If not handled with care, someone might get hurt.

Chapter 9

Exposing Hydrick's Psychic Demonstrations

MY FIRST ORDER OF BUSINESS AFTER I RETURNED TO DALLAS WAS TO ASSEMble a crew to help me shoot the exposé. My efforts were hampered when my producer backed out because of the "whole experience." I finally hired a six-foot, three-inch cameraman, Jim Carroll, and his technician, Roddy Bell. They had a personal interest in this story because their friend, Don Harris, formerly a newsman with WFAA-TV in Dallas, was the newsman killed by Jim Jones's associates in Guyana. They were not intimidated by what we might confront.

Setting the Stage
I made many calls to Hydrick and George to keep alive the chance of

filming Hydrick. After persisting for several weeks, Hydrick finally agreed to a June 3 taping at his studio in Salt Lake, to be followed by a June 4 taping in Dallas.

In May, Hydrick made a trip to Egypt to attend an international convention of psychics. He traveled with Janice Schrock, his adopted mother, and Pat Flannigan, the author of *Pyramid Power*—a pop book of the late sixties that detailed how pyramid-shaped structures unleash vast amounts of energy. Although a best-seller, the book was later dismissed by the scientific community for lack of empirical evidence.

While in Egypt, Hydrick appeared before family members of the late Anwar Sadat and presented a number of demonstrations from his repertoire. The trip helped to bolster his confidence, putting him more at ease for our shoot.

The basic strategy was to film Hydrick in Salt Lake on June 3 with restrictions that would make it impossible for him to display his "powers." These restrictions had to appear to be a natural part of the taping process in order not to arouse his suspicions. Then the next day, June 4, we would fly to Dallas for another taping session in a studio where the restrictions would be logically removed so that he would be free to make his demonstrations work. This way there would be no doubt in the viewer's mind how his tricks worked. I hoped that Hydrick would assume that the restrictions were removed because we were in a different location.

For the final convincer, I would then make the objects move. This would be done under the pretext that Hydrick could transfer his power through me. As described by Alex, Hydrick often let his students display *their* mental powers with his supervision, like the swinging bags; only he was the one who had control over moving the objects.

After he was exposed on camera, I hoped to send him back to Salt Lake, none the wiser, and then work to diffuse any potential physical threat if and when he found out. I didn't want anyone to get hurt during or after the taping—not Hydrick, those under his influence or anyone else. It was conceivable that if Hydrick found out, he might vent his anger.

"Gung Fu" Martial Arts

The weather when we arrived in Salt Lake was ideal, about seventy degrees with clear skies.

Mike Martin was at the studio when we drove up. Attired in cutoffs and a yellow T-shirt, he shot a number of stills with his 35mm camera when we arrived which he hoped to use in a book he was writing about Hydrick—a project he never finished. He looked a bit disoriented and stayed for half an hour or so and then left. It was the last time I saw him.

To establish a positive atmosphere with Hydrick, we stayed on the gym floor and filmed several of his athletic demonstrations. He first went through a short presentation of his home-grown martial arts that he called "Gung Fu." He followed this with one-thumb pushups and his amazing leaps into the air, kicking the net of a basketball goal. Then he presented his speed test with the credit card. We then moved on to the pencil trick.

Aborted Tricks

Our sound man, Roddy, attached a highly sensitive lavaliere microphone to the lapel of Hydrick's karate-gi. We thought this might pick up the sound of his blowing. Hydrick anticipated that potential and requested that we turn on some Oriental music, "So I can relax and concentrate," he said. It was the same music he had playing in the background when he moved the pencils on our first visit. Then he asked that the volume be increased, "to shut off all noises from his mind."

But evidently he was convinced that the music was insufficient to cover his puffs of air without arousing suspicions because the pencils never moved.

The dollar bill gambit was stifled in another way. For this, Roddy removed the microphone from Hydrick's lapel but then applied a two-inch-wide strip of gaffers tape along the tank's edge, securing it to the table. "This is important," Roddy explained indifferently in keeping with the subdued character of a detailed technician, "because if we have to stop and change tapes, and the tank is moved to a slightly different position, when the footage is edited, it will be noticed. Then people will think that we doctored the footage." Hydrick seemed satisfied with the explanation, but not with the net result.

Always the supreme actor, and with no other option but to go ahead, he grimaced, furrowed his brow, and held his hands around the tank to unleash "the power." Several minutes passed, more frustration, and then he gave up. The dollar bill didn't budge.

After this failure, he conveyed the trepidation of someone who was cornered. Randi's earlier attempt to expose him undoubtedly loomed in the back of his mind. I suggested, "Don't worry. If you can always display your powers, it looks fake." He seemed to buy this.

He then concluded with the swinging bags stunt: his students convinced, as they lay face-up and eyes closed on the gym floor, that their meditation exercise energized the bags. By ending the day with a successful demonstration, he was once again at ease.

We then packed and anxiously flew back to Dallas. Rose, who accompanied Hydrick, constantly reassured him that "tomorrow will be better."

The Dallas Studio

The taping took place at the studio of a small production house, in Carrollton, a northern Dallas suburb. The week before, I had met with the crew to go over the critical shots. If even one were missed, it could undermine the effectiveness of the exposé. It's not like shooting a scripted movie where you have several takes. Here, you either get it as it happens or it's gone.

We started the taping with a short, nonthreatening interview. If Hydrick, attired in a black gi, sensed that he wasn't in control, he became flustered and panicky, and would peer around the room. Rose, always in sight, was his safety net when others didn't believe in him.

Several minutes into the interview, I asked Hydrick to perform his one-inch punch. As before, the force of the punch threw me back several feet. We waited to tape this in Dallas to give Hydrick the psychological edge of having physical control over me.

I then suggested that he try the pencil test again on the two-and-a-half-foot square coffee table in front of us. For the camera I emphasized that the pencils were mine and not Hydrick's and were therefore not gimmicked.

With the mike obstacle eliminated, Hydrick blew and the pencil turned. He knew he couldn't be caught by the mike. He was also confident that the camera would not detect any facial movement because there weren't any—the product of months of practice while in jail.

He then demonstrated a new wrinkle; he lined up three pencils next to each other. The distance between each delicately balanced pencil was about two inches.

"Some people say that I blow on the pencil," he said. "So I've got three next to each other. I'm only going to move the middle pencil. If I were blowing, they'd all move."

With a perfectly directed jet of air, only the middle pencil moved. The others didn't. One only has to try this a few times to see how difficult it is.

Hydrick then told me that he could transfer his power to me and suggested that we change seats. After we did, he held my hand and pretended that he was transferring his energy to me. Usually after ten or fifteen seconds, he will start to change the positioning of his body, as if in the throes of concentration. Then, when he is close enough to the table, and he senses his subject is really into it, he will blow on the pencil. When the pencil turns, the onlooker is then totally mystified.

Holding my hand in his, he said, "Okay, let me know when you feel a warm sensation," hoping to suggest something that I might feel in my mind's eye.

But before he maneuvered himself close enough to unleash his puff of air, I blew first. The pencil rotated. Hydrick froze and then suddenly lunged his head toward the table.

"That didn't seem like . . . did you feel something?" he asked, like he'd just stepped into a room where a creaky door swung shut behind him.

Quickly I suggested that we move on to the "attack" demonstration. He agreed. I didn't want to give him time to think about what had just happened. I hoped that he would think that a small gust of air in the studio was the culprit that made the pencil move. It wouldn't be the first time that a random flow of air turned an inanimate object for him.

Confidence Returned

The "attack" stunt was easily exposed without tempting Hydrick's naturally suspicious mind. One camera was trained on my right eyebrow. The videotaped record shows that when Hydrick said that I thought "attack," my eyebrow had just twitched slightly. The twitching of my eyebrow was deliberate. Then Hydrick missed twice in a row. Why? Because the eyebrow never moved, and he was forced to guess. Before moving on, I let him score one last success by twitching the eyebrow to restore his confidence. The camera recorded everything, so there would be no question later how he knew.

Confident that he was at ease, I then suggested that we try the dollar bill under the tank.

To be sure that the dollar bill "experiment" would work, I had shopped all over town to find a tank where, when inverted, one corner would not meet the table flush. I finally found one. The clerk, who let me search through her entire stock, thought that I was crazy. I took all her tanks, turned them upside-down one at a time on the pet shop floor, examining each one on my hands and knees. She never could figure out what I was looking for. I thought about trying to explain my actions, but I don't think *I* would have believed my story.

After I removed Hydrick's pencils from the table, I placed the tank on the wood surface in front of him so that the slightly raised corner—only cracked about a sixteenth of an inch above the table's surface—was positioned *away* from him so he couldn't blow on it. But counting on his sharp powers of observation, I was sure that he would see the raised corner.

We waited as the dollar, balanced on the head of the pin which was embedded in the small block of wood, settled, until it didn't move. During this time I emphasized that I had supplied everything and that all were free of trickery.

"As a matter of fact," I added, "we have taken a precautionary measure. We turned off the air conditioning, so there won't be any heating and cooling of the tank. You can see that the bill is not moving. Now you're going to attempt to make it rotate?"

"Yeah," he replied, "I'll try first of all to get it to turn this way."

Leaning over the tank from his chair, he pretended to generate a charge that would cause the bill to move. Because he couldn't access the raised corner under which he could slip his air currents, his efforts to move the dollar failed. "Glass is so hard to work through sometimes," he complained.

"How about if we turn it? Would that help you?" I asked as I turned the tank so the corner was within "puffing" distance.

"Yeah, maybe," he replied. Within ten seconds the bill came to life, freely rotating on the head of the pin. Hydrick released the jet of air at the table just in front of the corner.

"Now, let me see if I can transfer the power to you," he stated, relieved that he had succeeded with this test. We swapped seats as before, Hydrick holding my left hand, acting out his part.

After a minute or so and no movement, I asked, "Can I try it more toward the front here?"

"Yeah."

I moved closer to the targeted corner, and I released a puff of air, mimicking Hydrick's technique. I did this before Hydrick could maneuver himself into position to exhale an invisibly directed air current.

"See if it starts to go. . . ."

The bill started turning. Hydrick snapped back in surprise as if stung.

Hydrick tries to channel his "power" through Korem to make the dollar bill under the fish tank move.

Recovering, he said, "See, I can . . . see it's coming from your hand," referring to the imaginary force field, when, in fact, he had no idea why the bill was moving.

"Should I try and get it to go back the other way?" I asked.

Without losing his composure, Hydrick responded, "Yeah. All you have to do is just, uh, like pull . . . pull toward you. Yeah," timing his remark to the natural recoil action of the bill.

"This is work," I said.

"Yeah. It makes you sweat a lot," Hydrick said relieved it was over.

"You're even better at this than I am. Your powers are better than mine," he said, still puzzled over what had just happened. He thought it was just a fluke.

I quickly wrapped up the session. He and Rose were shuttled to the airport for their flight back to Salt Lake. Phase one was completed without a hitch. Hydrick's tricks had been recorded in a way that revealed their natural origins, and at no time did anyone directly or indirectly make him feel threatened. Planning for phase two started immediately.

I believed that, if carefully approached, he might confess on camera that his feats were just tricks. How easy was it for him to fool people and get them to believe he had powers? But more importantly, what was the relationship between his abusive past and his need to be a psychic? Hugh thought it was a long shot. To pull it off, Hydrick would have to be confronted. The confrontation took place two months later, though it was not what I had in mind.

An Unexpected Threat

Before I confronted Hydrick, I needed to shoot some supporting footage, so I hired a producer/director to assist. I stated in a preproduction meeting that no one was to use drugs on my crew. I should have known that I was in for trouble when he replied that it might not be realistic to get complete compliance from some of the people he wanted to enlist. Against my better judgment, I hired him anyway in order to quickly bring the project to completion before the budget ran out.

After six days of shooting, I realized that I should have trusted my instincts. The last three days he shot for me were a complete disaster, wasting thousands of dollars. In addition to forgetting to bring equipment, much of the footage was poorly lit, and segments in which I was lecturing before a live audience were not shot. Even the lab that regularly developed all his film conceded that he blew it. It was not a matter of artistic interpretation. The last three days had to be reshot.

When I dismissed him, I said I would pay him only for the first three days production costs and expenses and only his out-of-pocket expenses for the last three days. What he did next quickly made me forget our recent victory. He called the lab where the first three days of footage were vaulted and requested that he be sent the reels for his review. He made this request *after* he had been released, to which he later testified under oath.

Then, in a long-distance call a week after the footage was discovered missing, he threatened to tell Hydrick that Hydrick had been exposed unless I paid him the full amount for the shoot. He did this even though he knew Hydrick could be a danger to himself or others if his exposure were not delicately handled.

I had to seek legal redress before this whole matter was settled. But in the meantime, he didn't know that I was in close contact with the Salt Lake police. They suspected that Hydrick had received some stolen guns, including a .357 magnum.

I immediately called detective George Clegg, my contact with the Salt Lake police, who was assigned to Hydrick's case. I told him of the producer's threat. We both agreed that if the producer talked to Hydrick in an inflammatory manner, the situation could turn deadly. Clegg was not yet prepared to issue a warrant for his arrest, but the realization of his exposure combined with the potential of a felony conviction might push Hydrick over the edge. Clegg said Hydrick had once told him that he would never be taken alive if Clegg ever tried to arrest him on any charge. Neither of us knew if this threat was just more of the "legend" of James Hydrick or not. But in the Los Angeles County Jail, Hydrick had self-inflicted over thirty gashes in each arm with a razor blade. One psychiatrist described it as a "desperate plea for help."

Detective Clegg agreed that the best course of action was for me to confront Hydrick in a controlled environment and try to get him admit that he was not a psychic. Maybe with the help of someone Hydrick trusted, his paranoia could be partially tamed.

I phoned Hugh, brought him up to speed, and told him that I was going to confront Hydrick. Hugh told me that I better have my camera crew right there waiting, when I confronted him with the truth. He said that most people when asked to confess, will change their mind and back out if given time to think about it. Jim Carroll and Roddy Bell agreed to be on call. That was on August 3.

I took a chance that Alex and Lisa, the family Hydrick had stayed with for six months, would help. Alex didn't know that Hydrick had been exposed. But he was a man of genuine integrity; I told him what had happened and asked him to help. He agreed. He said that he would call James and arrange a meeting for the next day at his office at 11:00 A.M.

Hanging up, I then devoted the rest of the day listing every possible scenario that might develop and our options for response. That evening when my wife Sandy and I went to bed, we prayed for guidance and a clear mind. I fell asleep steeped in contemplation.

Chapter 10

Hydrick's Confession

H UGH AND I ARRIVED AT ALEX'S MODEST OFFICE IN SALT LAKE AT 10:00 A.M., one hour before Hydrick was to meet us. Alex worked in the legal affairs department for a local utilities company. After we exchanged greetings, I asked him how he thought Hydrick would respond.

"His first response is going to be complete denial, and then he'll be angry and hurt that he's being doubted and so forth. But ultimately, I think he will come around." A perceptive lawyer, Alex's evaluation proved to be correct. I then went over with Alex how I thought we should proceed when Hydrick arrived.

Jim and Roddy were on stand-by in Dallas if Hydrick agreed to a taped confession. Against Hugh's more experienced judgment, I felt that if Hydrick were going to give a substantive confession, he needed a chance to think about it. It was a risk, but I sensed Hydrick would follow through when he realized that he had been exposed.

Hydrick Arrives

A few minutes after 11:00 A.M., Hydrick entered Alex's office wearing jeans and a T-shirt. He shuffled his feet nervously and sat down. Alex opened the meeting.

"James, Dan and Hugh have something they want to talk to you about. I want you to listen carefully because I know that you will do the right thing. Now, listen carefully," he repeated. His tone was paternal and Hydrick listened attentively, his eyes darting back and forth at the players seated on each side of the desk.

"James," I began as I reached down and opened my brief case, "I want you to know that you are one of the cleverest men I have ever met when it comes to inventing tricks." I avoided any direct eye contact with him for several seconds to minimize the pressure of what I had to say. I wanted the realization of his exposure to unfold in as relaxed and conversational a manner as possible.

"I want to show you some books I have written and published." As I said this I removed some books on sleight of hand. The texts contained the exact instructions for many tricks and are accompanied by photographs.

As he leafed through the pages, I said, "I have spent a lot of years inventing tricks for magicians, and I want to tell you that I think you are one of the best at what you do."

I was hoping that he wouldn't have the same reaction to me after the dust settled that he had to Randi. This confrontation was being handled with the support of a person Hydrick trusted, Alex.

"What do you mean?" he said with a slight whine in his voice, as he glanced at the pages. "What are you talking about?"

"Just listen to him, James, with both ears. It's for your own good," Alex interrupted.

I then explained how he had been exposed and that I wanted him to do an interview with Hugh and me during which he would talk about his past and what had motivated him to claim to be psychic. When Hugh thought it appropriate, he provided calm reinforcement. Hydrick's left leg bounced up and down furiously. I thought he was going to bolt for the door.

"I don't know what you're talking about," he said defensively. "What do you want from me?"

"Listen, James, you need to burn this bridge behind you and get on with the rest of your life. You need to come clean. Listen to Dan," Alex sternly counseled.

Admitting the Truth

The tenor of the meeting continued like this, alternating between Hydrick's refusal to acknowledge the real state of affairs, and Alex and Hugh and I trying to reason with him. After almost an hour, he relented.

"Now you're not going to make me look like some cheap criminal, are you?" he asked me.

"Look, I want you to take some time today and tonight to think about what you want to tell me," I offered. "I am not out to make you look like a buffoon."

Hydrick seemed convinced. After a few more minutes of discussion, he left and we hoped he'd come back.

The interview was to be held at 2:00 P.M. in a suite at the downtown Hilton. I would have preferred Hydrick's gym, but I didn't want to risk any unexpected intrusions that would scare him off. That afternoon and evening, Hugh and I prepared for the interview. The next day, Saturday, August 4, was one of the most exciting days of my life—and most frightening.

His Confession

Hydrick did show up.

The interview started a few minutes past 2:30 P.M. and lasted about two and a half hours. The weather had turned cold and was drizzling outside, so the taping was confined to our rented suite. What follows are excerpts from that interview.

This was the first time that someone with wide notoriety who claimed to have psychic or supernatural powers had consented to giving a taped confession.[1]

Hugh started the questioning.

Aynesworth: The real legend of James Hydrick isn't the legend that we have seen on TV and that we've read a lot about. But there really is a legend here, and it's perhaps even more bizarre and unusual than we knew. Tell us, James, who you really are.

Hydrick: My mother was in South Carolina or Georgia. And . . . I was abandoned when I was about three months old, in Graniteville, South Carolina; and from that time . . . on I was just placed in institutions, you know, foster homes and things . . . constantly. Why, I have no idea.[2]

Aynesworth: Well, tell me more about that abandonment. . . . You were thrown in a trash can? [Referring to a unconfirmed newspaper account.]

Hydrick: Yeah. Well, I was found in the trash can in Graniteville by the . . . I guess the Graniteville Sheriff's Department. Or, I think it was the trash department. I'm not really sure. As far as other abandonments . . . there were several ones. My mother was a heroin addict [not true], so I was born addicted to heroin and, you know, . . . I guess it was rough for me to deal with not having heroin. . . . Anyway, I survived, naturally, but what I had to go through wasn't really that . . .

[At this point his voice trailed off. At the beginning of the interview when a painful subject was broached, Hydrick frequently invented stories in which there was often a root of buried truth. Being found in a trash can was just one of many allegorical examples. For him, being "dumped" by his mother was the same as being thrown in a trash can.]

Korem: James, how do you know that you were abandoned in a trash can?

Hydrick: Well, because the police that dealt with me later told me. My grandmother told me about it. Apparently my father and mother had a blow-up, and my father was on the chain gang at the time in Aiken County. And she wasn't going to keep me, and she just put me in the trash can.[3]

Aynesworth: Did you ever see her after she abandoned you?

Hydrick: Yeah. Once or twice. She said she had to do it.

Aynesworth: How old were you?

Hydrick: Seventeen. You see, the majority of my abuse came from females. And . . . I got to the point where I couldn't feel pain. I mean, I used to have to bite myself and hit myself to cry so that they'd stop.

[His story that he bit his arm may have been devised to cover the fact that he sliced up both forearms on more than one occasion with a razor blade to draw attention to himself.

Then, as was consistent during the entire two and a half hours, he would candidly pull back the veil and recount what actually happened. He recalled abuse from his stepmother, Mary.]

Hydrick: I said it many a time, "So why was I born? Why were you born?" In fact, I mentioned before to my mother [stepmother]. . . . I had to make myself feel normal. So I used to call her "Mother," and she would always say, "I'm not your mother. Don't ever call me mother." But these things . . . they destroy, you know? I'd just rather not talk about it.

[Hydrick also called Janice Schrock, who adopted him only a few months before the interview, "Mother." Possibly she was a surrogate after being rejected by two childhood mothers.]

Aynesworth: So how did you get back? You must have retaliated or something.

Hydrick: I couldn't retaliate. I was too young. There was no way to retaliate.

Korem: Do you remember your childhood real well, or just . . . ?

Hydrick: A lot I don't remember because, you know, I suffered a lot of head injuries from my father, and a lot of it just . . . well, I try to

remember it and it hurts, you know, mentally. A lot of these things . . .
it does a lot of damage to me.

Korem: Hurts you inside?

Hydrick: Yeah. And I can't really talk about them. But you see, like
there were times when I would try to work things out with them. I'd
try to please her, and she'd just . . . I don't know . . . awful things. What's
the question again?

[Whenever Hugh and I probed deeper into his relationship with his
immediate family, Hydrick became confused and lost his train of
thought. We then inquired about his fantasy world.]

Hydrick: I don't even remember half of our neighbors. Except I was
unable to communicate with other kids. In fact, I remember at Reynolds
Pond, there were a lot of alligators there. My mother [stepmother]
threatened to throw us in there if we ever opened our mouth again. And
those were big 'gators; those suckers were bigger than the boat my
daddy was in.

Korem: Is that where you made up the fantasy about being used as
alligator bait?

Hydrick: Yeah. See, I'll always think of something worse happening,
so I'll be able to deal with it.

I had to create some type of fantasy that would make the beating not
hurt so bad.

[We then asked about his imagined Chinese mentor, Master Wu,
reminiscent of a major character from the television show "Kung Fu,"
who was portrayed as a wise old master.]

Hydrick: Well, the type of Master Wu that I conjure up was . . . when
my parents would lock me in a closet so I couldn't come out because
I suppose I embarrassed them. So . . . I closed my eyes and I was
actually picturing things coming up. I pictured myself being in a big
huge house, or mansion, monastery in China somewhere. It seemed like
astral projection,[4] like I was actually there. I could hear things taking
place.

And then I started seeing things. I wasn't really familiar with martial arts at the time, but I could actually see these people doing exercises with their hands and stuff. It was so strange. Every time I'd go into this thing, I'd hear a "dong!" And then when I'd appear, everybody would bow to me; and I'd be welcomed to come in.

[One of Hydrick's teacher's noted that his attention would wane in class unless the subject was magic or outer space. When he was nine years old, he was put in a juvenile home in Florence, South Carolina, and then transferred to an institutional school in McCormick, South Carolina. In McCormick he witnessed his first magic show presented by the magician, Harry Blackstone, Jr. The performance sparked his interest to learn some simple tricks. As we talked about that show, for the first time during the interview he generated genuine enthusiasm.]

Hydrick: Well, I guess I was about nine years old and I was in an institution, John De La howe, and that's when I saw Blackstone. In fact, I'm the one that went up and volunteered to do this little thing with him.

Korem: What was the trick that he did?

Hydrick: He had three oranges. He'd get a dollar bill from the audience. And then they would take the dollar bill, and he'd roll it up. He'd do something . . . I forget. It's been years. But anyway, the dollar bill would wind up inside the orange.

Korem: Did you think it was a good trick?

Hydrick: Yeah, I thought it was fascinating.

Korem: And you figured it out?

Hydrick: Yeah, I found out right there . . . Naturally, no dollar bill's going to grow in an orange.

Korem: (Laughter)

Hydrick: If it is, show me where the tree is! (More laughter)

[Hydrick then described his amazement at how easily people are fooled.]

Hydrick: Blackstone would take and ball up a thing of paper. And all of a sudden, he'd move his hands around and throw the paper over the guy's head. And everybody in the audience is laughing, and this guy's going, "Now, what are they laughing at?" And he opened his hand, and the guy goes like that . . . [Hydrick mimes a startled expression]. And it's just a sleight of hand. The guy's paying attention to the hand movement and actually he'd thrown the paper over his head.

Things like that impressed me, how close-minded a lot of people were. It's so fascinating to see how people would just miss things—just like that. The obvious things, they'd miss.

Korem: And you found that you were able to spot the obvious.

Hydrick: Yeah. Well, for some reason, I could always spot how it was done.

[It turned out that as youngsters we both were awed by the skills of Harry Houdini. When I was in grade school, I used the name Houdani.

When teaching kids about the difference between good tricks and bad tricks, I point out that magic tricks are *good* tricks as long as they are presented as tricks and nothing more. There is nothing inherently evil in fooling someone, like a trick play in sports. What's important is how the trick is used, a lesson Hydrick never learned as a youngster.]

Korem: I started doing magic when I was nine. I bought a couple of books. But I know that you didn't know how to read and write. How did you learn?

Hydrick: I read about this magician, Harry Houdini, and it told about certain tricks that he did. They were good tricks, and nobody could ever figure them out. And what I'd do was . . . I learned to read a little bit . . . and I'd con my teachers into reading to me.

Korem: How'd you do that?

Hydrick: Just guess I'd have that sweet little voice. Miss King used to read for me. She was a real good teacher. When she used to read for me, I'd just sit back and think . . . You got all those magicians who make rabbits disappear and Harry Houdini makes an elephant disappear.

So I tried to figure out the obvious thing, and I was right! Harry Houdini had a box that looked like a triangle, but it wasn't. There was another piece to it. And actually, when he closed the curtains, it turned, so the elephant's actually behind.

It was something I'd figure out. And I was right. And then I'd say, "Well geez, if people go crazy over that, maybe I should do something people would go crazy over." But then I didn't work on things. I got into UFOs.

[Hydrick related that he first started doing his "power" tricks when he was committed to Whitten Center—an institution for the mentally retarded, even though he was not retarded.]

Hydrick: I wanted attention. My parents would never give it to me. I would always be ignored or kicked around. And I'd have to do this to make me feel good. It gave me confidence. Everytime someone thought what I did was very good, but I'd never tell them it was [a trick]. I'd tell them something else. Because if I told them it was, they'd say, "Oh fine, it's just a trick." But I'd always tell them it was something else so that I continued to get recognition.

Aynesworth: You were on "That's Incredible" a few months back. You tricked them.

Hydrick: Tricked the whole world.

Aynesworth: You tricked them really good. Do you remember how impressed they were with you? What did it make you feel like?

Hydrick: It's like a hand reaching out for recognition. I guess I just wanted to be known. I needed to be recognized. All my life I've been . . . and I hate to keep going back, but . . . I don't know. I just wanted to see how open-minded people were. I wanted to see if these people were really intelligent and I was really dumb. My whole idea behind this in the first place was to see how dumb America was, how dumb the world is. I mean if doctors put children in institutions . . . to put a kid in an institution, you might as well bury him alive.

Korem: You wanted to show them that if they thought you were retarded, you could still fool them. Was that it?

Hydrick: See, that's the thing. It's so funny. I am retarded. [Sarcastic.] Six years I stayed in a mental institution. Six years! I was put on Melaril and Thorazine so they could control me. I . . . so many things bad were done, you know, that could have destroyed me. All these doctors that

James Hydrick became the first widely known psychic to confess on camera how and why he was able to seemingly convince others that he possessed powers.

I went through said, "Yes, he is retarded; put him in a school. He's no good for the public." All I'm saying is: "Hi, dummy. Look where I am now." You see? I'm not . . . you know, I'm not retarded. Do you think I'm retarded? Do you think I have a low I.Q.?

Korem: Me, personally?

Hydrick: Yeah.

Korem: No. Do you feel that I'm trying to hurt you?

Hydrick: No.

Korem: Why?

Hydrick: Why would you hurt me? Why? You tell me.

Korem: Well, you've had many other people hurt you in your life. Why would you say that Dan Korem, who you've only met a few times . . . why would you say that I'm not that kind of person?

Hydrick: I just don't feel that way . . . James Randi, he's so against . . .

[I changed the subject to diffuse his anger. Randi later sent me a letter expressing regret that he didn't know Hydrick's past before confronting him. He compassionately offered his assistance to Hydrick if he would accept it.

Hydrick then talked about some of the techniques that he mastered in jail which he used to move objects.]

Hydrick: See, it takes so many years of practice in getting this down pat [laughs and slaps his hands together] . . . to where you can't see my mouth move when I blow. And what I'd do is I'd grab the hand [grabs my hand] and I'd do like this [exhales jet of air and turns head] and it's already moved because I can direct it in a way to where it hits right on every time. And in my practice—you know, I spent a year and six months in solitary confinement. All the time I thought and thought, and finally said to myself, "That's it. That's what I'm going to do." [Visibly excited.]

Korem: And you could take all the time you wanted to learn how to breathe and . . . ?

Hydrick: Right.

Korem: . . . make them move?

Hydrick: Right. And I spent hours and hours holding my breath, and breathing . . . different breath controls. And I could make deputies think someone touched them on their neck or something. I could breathe one way but be looking over here, and they'd feel something. And I'd say [whispering], "That's a ghost." And they'd faint right there on the floor. [Laughs.] You see, it's something that got me recognition. [They'd say,] "That guy's possessed."

[While in prison, Hydrick was befriended by a priest, Brother Gerald, earlier referenced. He taught him how to read and write and assisted in his parole to Salt Lake. He was a positive role model for Hydrick. Most of the male role models whom Hydrick respected were each caring people with strong moral or Christian convictions. These included Frank Galardi, a crime prevention officer in Aiken, S.C., noted for his volunteer work with Prison Fellowship, a ministry started by Chuck Colson; Alex in Salt Lake; and Brother Gerald, the chaplain at the jail. Each was a solid citizen and had an accurate picture of the "real" James Hydrick. It is likely that it was his relationship with these men that kept him from going completely over the edge. He at least gravitated toward the right kinds of people—those who would call him to the mat when he tried to take advantage of them. Although he expressed great hatred toward institutions, he respected genuine authority. Every law enforcement person and prison official made this observation. But their influence didn't stop him from using his crutch, miracle-like tricks, to attain recognition. He took Brother Gerald's advice on how to "turn people from bad to good," and twisted the essence of Brother Gerald's beliefs.]

Hydrick: I was always into helping people. And there'd be inmates that were so mean, but they were good. I saw this side of them.

I used to go to Brother Gerald [and ask him], "How do you convert people? How do you get them to go from bad to good?" And he would tell me, "Well, you've got to turn them on to Jesus." And he gave me a Bible and I started reading about Jesus . . . how Jesus would heal. A lot of things that he did was by the power of suggestion.

So I say, "Hmm, I got an idea." So I didn't tell Brother Gerald this, but I would convert twenty inmates a day. I'd start telling them about Jesus and stuff, and I'd read things, and they'd get interested. And then when they started to get turned off, I'd say, "Hey, check this out, man. You don't believe it exists? If the Lord is here with me, make the pages move."

Korem: What would happen?

Hydrick: I'd open the Bible and I'd say, "Father, in the name of Jesus Christ, make these pages move. And pheaoo! [Makes sound and mimes page turning over.] The guy's going "Uh, oh." You know it worked every time. Then I'd say, "It's in you." I'd say [gibberish]. They had something they called it. It's where you speak in a . . .

Korem: Speaking in tongues.

Hydrick: Tongues . . . where you go [more invented gibberish]. I watched this guy on TV who would be speaking about Christ and stuff.

And he'd go . . . [gibberish]. He was a really good actor. And I'd do like
he did and I'd tell the guy, "I gotta call the Lord and see if you can get
him to do this. But you are going to have the power to do this, if you
accept the Lord." And the next thing you know, you'd see this guy wearing
a big cross, passing out Bibles to people.

[When in Egypt, Hydrick related how he "healed" a woman believed
to be stricken with a heart attack. He convinced here of his powers with
his tricks and then her mind did the rest. Although not well known to
laymen, there are various medical conditions that are psychosomatic in
origin which can create the same sensation as a heart attack, without
damaging the heart. The origin of the symptom is in the mind and not
physically in the heart cavity. Certain physical ailments like a hiatal
hernia can also mimic the sensation of a heart attack. In addition,
people under great stress sometimes complain of chest pain, when
there is no real threat of a heart attack—although this should not keep
one from checking out chest pains with the doctor.]

Hydrick: I'm telling you, it's the power of suggestion. Because this
lady has seen me perform so much, same thing with Jesus Christ . . . the
power of faith . . . the belief. She strongly believed that I could actually
heal her and she came right up.

Korem: What did you do that made her believe that?

Hydrick: By moving things. And I would show her so many things and
I would touch her, and she'd actually feel weird things. But it's only in
her mind. She wanted to feel these things.

[Here Hydrick gives the thinking person a chilling warning. Just because a person uses the name of Christ does not give their claims of
miracles credibility. What gives the claims credibility is simply if the
reports are true. What this woman experienced was similar to what
Hydrick's friend, Rose, described as a "shot of electricity." When errone-
ous reports abound and this kind of activity runs amok, the result is what
can appear to be a cult; or even worse, an actual cult.]

Korem: Do you think that people, watching this particular program,
might think that what you were trying to start was a cult?

Hydrick: Yes. See, the only type of person that would have powers, like I claimed to have had, would have been some type of anti-Christ or god. But when they go putting it over on the public, they're doing it for one reason: that reason is to get a cult so they have power and authority over people. Dan, if you didn't do what you did, I would never have come out.

Korem: Why not?

Hydrick: Because I wanted to see how far I could take it.

Korem: Okay, but let me ask you this: you say that you did not want to start a cult?

Hydrick: [Right.]

Korem: Now you know that you can [barely] read or write and that you lack an education.

Hydrick: Right.

Korem: Do you think the possibility existed that somebody could have used you to form a cult?

Hydrick: Absolutely. Kurbegovic . . . Muharem Kurbegovic, who was the Alphabet Bomber who blew up the airport in L.A., he wanted to use me for a cult. . . . Sirhan Sirhan, who was part of the occult—it's called Aliens of America, the AOA. These people wanted to use me as a leader of their cult.

Korem: How did they want to use you?

Hydrick: To brainwash people . . . by showing them this power and saying that this power came from something that it didn't.

Korem: Were adults fooled more by what you did?

Hydrick: Absolutely. In fact there were more adults fooled than children.

Korem: Why?

Hydrick: Because a lot of adults are looking for something like this. They *want* to believe that something like this exists.

[Hydrick's story about the AOA, Kurbegovic, and Sirhan Sirhan were never substantiated, and were most probably invented, although he showed me cultic writings which he said were distributed by Kurbegovic. But there were those who did want to introduce him to cult-like communities where he could be used to increase a following.]

Aynesworth: You love to work with kids. Why do you suppose that is?

Hydrick: Well, being with kids . . . any time I'm around children, it's like I've found a missing piece from my life. See I wasn't able to be around kids my own age, so I have to be around kids so that I'm comfortable. If I'm always around adults, it's like something's missing. It makes me feel good inside to be around kids; I love kids. When I see a kid, I see happiness. I see love. I see laughter, joy, and intelligence.

Korem: When do you feel uptight?

Hydrick: I never . . . I have no reason to feel uptight.

Korem: There are times when I've been with you and you really felt uptight. Lisa said that when you first came to their house, it was like watching an animal that was all caged up inside and you just . . . you couldn't sit down. When do you feel at ease?

Hydrick: I can never feel at ease.

Korem: Why?

Hydrick: Because my natural instinct is not to be at ease. I mean, I can't be at ease. I wish I could. When I'm around children I'm calmed down.

[I then asked him about love—the most basic and essential of the human needs, to give and receive.]

Korem: What do you think it means to love someone?

Hydrick: To know them, to care, to feel for them. When I love someone, I care for them. I want to be with them. I want to help them in all that I can. I want to share my life with them. But see, my type of love . . . I can't share my life with other people because it's not a normal life.

Korem: When was the last time you told someone you loved them?

Hydrick: I don't tell people I love them. I've never told anyone I loved them.

Korem: Never?

Hydrick: So many times when I was living with Alex and Lisa, she would sort of hug me to let me know she loves me. And I would reject it. I can't stand to be touched. But it's not because I don't like people. Because I'm afraid. You see? And I can't love someone . . . or tell them I can love, but I can't tell them because I don't recognize, I don't identify with the word *love.* And to me, love . . . it's a trick.

Korem: Is there anything else you'd like to say on camera?

Hydrick: I apologize to the American people. If they were taken in by what I've done, if I actually fooled them, then I was wrong.

Chapter 11
The Arrest

HYDRICK'S DEMEANOR CHANGED IN THE HOTEL SUITE WHEN I ASKED HIM TO conclude the interview by demonstrating one last trick for the camera—the page-turning trick, the same trick James Randi tried to expose. Instantly, Hydrick lashed out at his memory of Randi, the "man of hatred," as he called him.

The next moment he bounced back bragging that he could blow in such a way that not even the lavaliere mike could pick up his puffs of air. But when I asked him to demonstrate this technique, he became agitated. He knew it couldn't be done, but he tried in spite of the impossibility. His first two attempts to turn the pages were unsuccessful: he wasn't exhaling enough air to turn the pages.

Jim, our cameraman, requested that he try again. Hydrick balked. He shifted uncomfortably in his chair. He was self-exposing his last trick. It was finished. The weight of the moment pressed hard on him.

"You've already done it twice," I offered.

Seated at a table with the opened phone book before him, he complained, "This ain't right. Something's not right. I don't know, man. This just isn't cool at all. Look, just forget the part about Randi. I don't want to do it," he said despondently with a tinge of anger. He closed the book with a look of disgust.

The relaxed atmosphere turned tense. One more time Jim coaxed Hydrick to try and turn the page over. Hydrick tried. The page didn't turn, it merely fluttered at its edges. The microphone clearly picked up his blowing. Angrily he slammed his fist on the heavy table, almost turning it over.

We quickly ended the session.

An Anxious Night

Alex helped calm Hydrick down. Small talk broke out, and we decided to meet for dinner in a couple of hours.

Refreshed, we all ordered steaks. Hydrick ordered a large T-bone which he primitively cut into four pieces and devoured in four bites. Lisa said she was the first to teach him how to use a knife and fork properly.

After dinner, Hydrick pulled an airline ticket out of his pocket. It was for a September 25 flight to London—a little over two weeks away—and he spoke of moving out of the country. When we finished our desserts, we parted without much conversation. He kept telling me, "I just feel something is wrong. I need to get around some kids to get my spirits up."

Hugh and I worked until 11:00 P.M. comparing notes, and then we both turned in.

At 1:00 A.M. I was awakened by a call from Detective Clegg. He asked me how the taping went. After I told him, he said that he was looking for Hydrick, and that he was going to arrest him that night on second degree felony charges for breaking and entering. He believed Hydrick still had in his possession the .357 magnum.

Clegg also informed me that earlier that evening, after Hydrick left the Hilton, he had gone to see one of his students. But the child's parent had refused to let Hydrick in the house, and Hydrick had threatened the parent.

Clegg thought that it would be best if I changed rooms and registered under an assumed name. He said the parent described Hydrick's behavior as "desperate."

I went downstairs and gave a description of Hydrick to the security guard in the lobby and instructed him to call the police if he saw Hydrick. Hydrick often fantasized about being a modern-day *ninja*, the legendary martial arts assassins who cloaked themselves in black.

I realized that the combination of his exposure and, if he caught wind of it, his imminent arrest, might trigger Hydrick to retaliate against me. I stayed awake until 3:00 A.M. peering out the window for his white Camaro that never materialized.

Around 4:00 A.M. Hydrick was arrested without incident.

A Final Stunt

Even when in jail, his world of illusion continued. A few days after his arrest, a deputy passed by his cell and saw the twenty-two-year-old Hydrick hanging from the neck in the noose of a rope. He shouted for help. Hydrick laughed.

"I tied a noose around my neck, got up on my tiptoes and rocked back and forth like I had hanged myself. It was really funny," he chuckled as he recounted the jailer's fright.

"It was just another trick?" I asked when I visited him in jail. My question echoed off the sickly green painted concrete walls.

"Yeah, just another trick. Something to pass the time."

The following year Hydrick escaped twice from confinement. The second escape took place on October 23, 1982. Both times, I was the

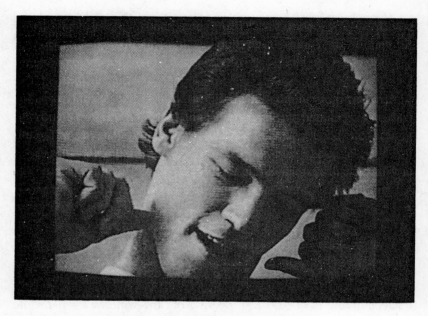

Hydrick describes how he performed his mock hanging while in jail.

first person that he called. He always told me he liked me. Perhaps this
was because he respected me for never attacking him as a person, only
his claims of power.

He was eventually caught and served his time. In 1985 he migrated
back to Aiken where he served another year for failing to pull his car
over when he was signaled by a local police officer. He was released
in March of 1987. Later that same year he married, was reincarcerated
for a minor parole violation and divorced.

During this last incarceration, he was confined to a cell on death row
in South Carolina because of his numerous escapes from prisons and
jails in Utah, Georgia and South Carolina (from 1982-86). He resorted
to breaking out of handcuffs and even kicking down a jail wall in the
Richmond County Jail in Georgia where he was held on a burglary
charge.

Hydrick on his release from prison and hopefully to a better life.

In December 1987, Hydrick walked free from the Watkins Pre-Release Center in Columbia, South Carolina, with a check for $11,000 in settlement of a suit for wrongfully being imprisoned on death row for safekeeping.

"Hydrick was supposed to be picked up in style—in a stretch limousine paid for by a promoter in Atlanta who is setting up kick boxing fights for Hydrick (now twenty-eight and two-hundred-forty pounds) and a video of his martial arts and telekinetic skills. But the promoter failed to come through and Hydrick's chauffeur was a bail bondsman he befriended while working as a bounty hunter" (AP report 12-2-87).

The legend of James Hydrick continues.

In April of 1988 he called me and offered to help do surveillance work in a case I was working on related to deviant sexual crimes committed by a Satanic cult.

He said, "Dan, I like you and your work and I want to help you." It was this part of James Hydrick which sporadically surfaced that rallied people like Alex to help him.

What does the future hold for him? I don't know. It seems that he is far less of a threat to himself and others now than when I met him, and he no longer pretends to be a psychic. I hope that with time he will learn how to live with his past. Regardless of what happened to him, he is still responsible for his actions. He knows that. I just hope he believes it.

The tragic nature of his story can be summarized by his mother Lois's response when she was asked if she would have done anything differently. Her tearful reply was that she would have stayed with her abusive husband to keep the family together. "He was a good husband, he was a good provider . . . he just happened to be a wife beater."

When we asked Lois if she knew that Billy had finally gotten off the booze and had become a "born-again Christian," she said, "Yeah, but he was born again too damn late."

Hydrick often said, "I want to do something to stop child abuse." His wish was realized when the Department of Health and Human Resources purchased my documentary, "Psychic Confession," to help instruct social workers on the effects of child abuse.

Desire for Power

The devastation of Hydrick's family and subsequent abuse chiseled out a mindset that believed "love is a trick," and spun him into a fantasy world where another basic human need—recognition—became a perverted pursuit.

With a clever mind, he found recognition by feeding off of a cultural desire to have and believe in one's own personal powers: "Because a lot of adults are looking for something like this. They *want* to believe that something like this exists."

Even though Hydrick must remain accountable for his actions, each of us is accountable to discern the truth. If a person can convince others that they have powers and can tie it into a religious belief—no matter how cavalier or spontaneously it's put together—there is an increased possibility that such a person could adroitly be used to form a cult.

Someone I was never able to fully help was Mike. After the first taping, I never saw him again. He discontinued his contact with Hydrick and has been up and down since. His brother Rob, who had believed that Hydrick was demon possessed, later changed his perspective after viewing "Psychic Confession" which aired nationally in 1983.

Clips from "Psychic Confession" continue to air each year, and it has been sold for viewing to a number of foreign television markets. It's a story suspended in time on video tape, and I hope it continues to be a reminder of our need to be discerning.

Part IV
Magic, Magi and Seers from the East

Chapter 12

Old Testament Perspectives

HYDRICK INSTINCTIVELY REALIZED AND CAPITALIZED ON THE CONNECTION BE-tween claims of psychic or supernatural powers and spiritual be-liefs. When he convinced his onlookers of his powers, it provided an entrée to expound on *how* he developed his powers and from *where* they originated. Those who witnessed Hydrick's pseudo-teleki-netic abilities often listened to his spiritual explanations in the hope that they too could develop the same skills. Some believed him outright. Others (although skeptical of his explanations) listened to his explana-tions because they couldn't offer a better unified theory. But the goal both camps sought was the same: to have their own *personal* power.

Illusions and Powers

When I lecture and present demonstrations on this subject, regardless of the setting, the questions always turn to those of a spiritual nature. The reason is inherent in the subject matter. Questions such as: Can we develop powers independent of outside forces, or is there really something out there beyond ourselves which can enable this to happen? Is there a good supernatural power and is there an evil supernatural power, or is there simply a neutral "force"—or neither?

My personal belief is that the Christian version concerning the question of powers is the one that is accurate: God is the author of good supernatural powers and Satan is the perpetrator of evil supernatural powers. However, as a journalist I have encountered very few verifiable cases of real supernatural powers in relation to the number of reports that I receive. Even though I believe in the supernatural realm—and am not inclined to dismiss the possibility when investigating a case—morally and ethically I am bound to report the facts.

When it comes to *human* psychic abilities, however, I do not believe that they exist at all because I have never seen any convincing or authoritative evidence for their existence. If and when verifiable evidence surfaces, I will gladly change my position. Accepting the truth in no way threatens my professional obligations or personal beliefs.

Many years ago, a Christian woman gently admonished me and said, "Magic is of the devil and you shouldn't be doing those tricks." As I was relatively new to the faith, her statement shocked me. I couldn't figure out what was wrong with sleight-of-hand tricks, like making a coin disappear and reappear, if everyone knew they were tricks. A trick is not something that is supernatural, but rather an ingenious feat designed to puzzle or amuse people. When I perform a trick, audiences are aware that I am there to entertain, not to convince anyone of real powers.

When one creates an illusion, it simply creates a mistaken idea or impression in someone's mind, which in itself is not necessarily a bad thing. The kindly woman who confronted me was herself the creator of an illusion. By wearing make-up, she tried to give the impression that she was younger than her actual age. Men who use hair treatments "to make that gray fade away" do the same thing.

Motive, Method and Consequence
A skillful film director also uses illusions. The most pronounced are 3-D movies where the action on the screen looks like it's really coming into your lap. This is another example of an illusion where the intent is not to inflict harm, but to entertain.

However, if a news director used actors to create the illusion of a live news story without informing the viewer, then that would be unethical. The trust factor between the news organization and the viewer has been violated because we expect TV news to report real events.

To determine if it is acceptable to use a particular deception or illusion in a given situation, one must examine the motive (why a deception is used), the method chosen and the consequence of using a deception. As explained (although most of us never think of make-up as a type of deception while it is), deception itself is not necessarily a bad thing.

Examining the motive, method and consequence is not situational ethics which holds that, for example, adultery is sometimes wrong and sometimes isn't. Adultery is adultery and is always wrong. By examining these three factors, however, we can determine if the deception chosen is being used in a way that is good or harmful.

When a drug agent goes undercover to crack a drug ring, we don't object when he has to deceive ring members into believing that he is one of them. (As one professor of philosophy told me, "A lie is withholding the truth from someone who has a right to know.") The motive for the agent's use of deception is to capture the criminal. This is good. His method is to pretend that he is someone that he isn't. Again no one is harmed except the felon. And the consequence is that the supply of drugs will be curtailed which could save someone's life. Therefore his use of deception—using a fake I.D.—is ethical.

Now if the agent decides to use a nine-year-old girl as a decoy who could be killed, then his method is unsuitable and the deception shouldn't be used because an innocent person could be harmed.

Even in the Bible there are numerous examples in which tricks or illusions were not only used, but in which those who used them by faith were rewarded by God.

In the first chapter of Exodus the Hebrew midwives wouldn't kill the Hebrew baby boys at birth as ordered by Pharaoh. They tricked Pharaoh by offering the explanation that the Hebrew mothers had their babies so quickly that they couldn't get there in time for the delivery. It's recorded that they were rewarded by God for their deception. The *motive, method* and *consequence* of their actions were all acceptable and appropriate.

From an educational perspective, I have found that a really puzzling trick is one of the best ways to confront an audience with the concept that all of us are vulnerable to being deceived. People have actually thanked me for fooling them because a baffling trick was the catalyst that drove home the point. From this perspective, I wanted to know if the woman who chastised me for doing tricks was correct or mistaken.

The Biblical Record

To explore this further, I looked up the Old Testament word for *magic.* It is the Hebrew word *hartōm,* which means "one who draws circles," referring to an astrologer, one who tries to predict the future by studying the stars and horoscopes. *Hartōm* is derived from the word *heret,* which means scribe. It is usually mentioned in connection with wise men, the *hakāmîm* and the *mᵉkashpîm,* who whisper and cast spells. *Kashāp* is usually translated "sorcerer."

These definitions did not fit what I did: sleight of hand. I also discovered that up until several hundred years ago, laymen used to refer to such tricksters as jugglers, not magicians, because of our clever sleight-of-hand ability. No doubt it was because of an unscrupulous performer who swindled his audience into believing that what he was doing was not a trick but the result of a secret power that people started calling us magicians—thus the confusion between a sleight-of-hand performer and someone who claimed to have real powers.

In the late sixties and early seventies a stage magician named Kreskin claimed that he could read people's minds by using ESP. The talented performer is still quite popular today. In Chicago, during the summer of 1972, I met with Kreskin (whose real name is George Kresge) in his dressing room and told him that I was going to publicly expose how he did his tricks if he continued claiming they were mental powers.

You see, while in college I did a mentalism act similar to his to earn extra money. When I told people that it was a trick and not a power, many didn't believe me and said, "But you're doing the same kinds of things as Kreskin, and he says they are not tricks." When I refused to divulge the secret because of the code of ethics I agreed to uphold when I became a member of the International Brotherhood of Magicians (yes, there really is such an organization of over seventy-five hundred members worldwide), a typical response was, "See, you can't prove that he's doing tricks." Some even suggested that I was claiming they were tricks so "you can keep the secret of your powers to yourself." At the time I was nineteen years old. I was amazed at how anxious people were to believe.

Kreskin was irate when I challenged him and threatened to sue me for one million dollars. I didn't take him seriously since I could just see the headlines: "Famous Entertainer Sues College Student—Bicycle Repossessed!" He never did sue me, but within a short period of time he stopped claiming to have ESP. Occasionally he slips back into his old mode as indicated by an article in the September 3, 1987, *Dallas Morning News* where he said, "I pick up mental images of what's in other people's minds. Basically I perceive their thoughts. For years Dr. Margaret Meade used to say that she didn't want me to call myself a mentalist. She said, 'Kreskin, you are a sensitive.' I think she meant that I raise my ability to feel and perceive beyond the average person, just as someone can lose his sight in adult life and develop an extraordinary sense of hearing."

What Kreskin does as a performer is entertaining, but when he makes this kind of a statement, he causes confusion. In addition he lends credibility to others who claim they have powers.

Kreskin's *motive* when using illusion and tricks is to entertain and earn a good living. This is fine. Part of his *method* or vehicle—to use well-known and some not so well-known magician's tricks—is also all right. What isn't acceptable is the false impression he creates by not stating that he uses trickery. The *consequences* of his deliberately misleading an audience to believe that what he does is anything other than a trick is that some really believe he has some kind of mind power. While Kreskin avoids specific terms like *mind powers* and *E.S.P.,* he does create the illusion in the spectator's mind—as indicated in the interview—that he relies on something more than the five senses and astute thinking.

Confusing real powers with cleverly constructed illusions is not something that is new. What follows are a few biblical examples beginning with Moses' encounter with the magicians of Pharaoh's court as recorded in the book of Exodus in the Old Testament.

Pharaoh's Magicians

Earlier I mentioned that the Egyptian Pharaoh demanded that all the male babies of the Hebrews be killed at birth. Moses, however, escaped death because his mother disobeyed the command, putting him in a watertight basket that she placed in the reeds along the bank of the Nile. Moses' sister then stood guard to see what would happen. Pharaoh's daughter came to bathe, noticed the basket and took Moses into her home, raising him as her own.

Many years later, Moses killed an Egyptian overseer who was beating a Hebrew slave. He then fled from Egypt to the land of Midian. There it is recorded that the Lord appeared to him in the famous "burning bush" passage in Exodus 3. The Lord said he had heard the cries of his people, who had been in bondage for over 400 years, and he instructed Moses to go to Pharaoh and tell him, "Let my people go!"

The Lord then told Moses to have his brother, Aaron, take Moses' staff and throw it to the ground where it would change to a snake; this was a sign that God, "I am," was behind the request (Exodus 3 and 4). Exodus 7:11-12 then states that the magicians in Pharaoh's court seemingly duplicated Moses' miracle, but that Aaron's staff (snake) swallowed up their staffs (snakes). Historians estimate this took place circa 1400 B.C.: "So Moses and Aaron went to Pharaoh and did just as the Lord commanded. Aaron threw his staff down in front of Pharaoh and his officials, and it became a snake. Pharaoh then summoned wise men and sorcerers, and the Egyptian magicians also did the same things by their secret arts: Each one threw down his staff and it became a snake. But Aaron's staff swallowed up their staffs" (Ex 7:10-12).

What's interesting is that the word used to describe the activity of the Egyptian magicians is the Hebrew word *lahaṭ,* which translates "secret arts" or "enchantments." It is derived from a word that means to wrap or envelop—as if to ensnare, to perform covertly. There is nothing to suggest in the derivation of the word, or its use in other passages, that it refers to real supernatural powers.

If the magicians changed the staffs to snakes by trickery and not by a power, they would have to either disguise the snakes as rods, conceal the snakes in something that looked like a rod or execute a switch. Is this possible for a skilled magician? I believe it is.

I once read an account that a cobra given a sharp crack behind the head would go rigid like a rod. This was supposedly a snake charmer's trick. If the snake in this state were then covered with dye, it could be made to look like a rod. I decided to check this possibility with the reptile curators at the San Diego Zoo, the Brookfield Zoo in Chicago and the Dallas Zoo. All are known for their expertise in herpetology. Susan Schaffer, at the San Diego Zoo, said that striking a snake to make it go rigid is a myth. As a matter of fact, she said, "The hardest thing to do is to stretch a snake out straight, which is the reason it is difficult to accurately measure their length." With this option ruled out, I pursued other possibilities.

The most practical method to duplicate the magicians' feat is similar to a trick performed today where a magician changes a cane to a silk handkerchief, rope or a handful of flowers. This method best fits the natural instincts of a snake.

Ms. Schaffer explained that to measure the length of a snake, she takes a tightfitting tube and coaxes the snake into it, as snakes like dark, tight-fitting environs. To replicate the illusion of changing a rod into a snake, a telescopic shell must be constructed to house the snake. Given the materials available during that time period, such as a piece of pliable papyrus, this could easily be made. With the snake concealed inside the "staff," the magician would simply have to pass his hand over the shell, collapsing it at the same time, leaving the snake in its place. This action could be covered by the motion of throwing the staff to the ground, creating the illusion that the staff visibly changes to a snake.

Another option—switching a real snake for a rod—would be possible if the staff were momentarily covered or hidden from view as it was being thrown down. One solution would involve having a small needlelike hook on the side of the staff near the top, while the snake is concealed in the baggy sleeves of the magician's tunic. To effect the switch, the magician would need to have an accomplice standing next to him.

As the magician lifts his staff to throw it down, his hand raises up behind his accomplice's back. Then, on his downward throwing motion, without hesitation, he engages the hook—fixed near the top of the staff—on the assistant's cloak leaving it hanging there out of sight. Completing his downward throwing motion, he releases the snake from his sleeve and the transformation is complete. The disadvantage would be that no one could be to the sides or behind the magician. For this reason, the first method would be best as it is self-contained, although many other methods could be invented to suit the situation.

The Ten Plagues

When Pharaoh wasn't impressed by Moses' miracle because of his magicians' handiwork, Moses was instructed by the Lord to inflict the land of Egypt with the first of ten plagues: changing the Nile into blood. When the magicians duplicated this plague, Moses then caused a multitude of frogs to infest the land. This was the last plague that the magicians duplicated by what I believe were illusions—not supernatural powers. After the second plague, their powers fail.

The third plague was an infestation of gnats. Logically, if the magicians had used supernatural powers to *create* frogs, a far more complex creature than a gnat, then they should have been able to conjure up gnats or flies which were the fourth plague. Something just doesn't seem right here.

Each of the first two plagues could easily have been reproduced on a small scale by trickery without calling on supernatural powers. A study of some elementary texts for magicians will reveal a number of alternatives.

A simple method to simulate changing water to blood is the following: A container of red dye is buried near the bank of the river, which in this case is the Nile. A line is then attached to the container to release the dye in the water. This line is then buried in the sand along the shore where an accomplice pulls and releases the dye. When one of the magicians goes to fetch a sample of the "blood," he can switch it for a cup or container of real blood. This is but one of many options that would produce the desired effect.

Producing frogs would have been even easier to negotiate. Magicians today produce live doves in the middle of a stage from handkerchiefs; and doves are far more difficult to handle than a docile frog. But gnats and flies aren't as easy to negotiate en masse. It would have been hard to collect and keep them alive. Frogs, on the other hand, would have been very easy to collect, which is the reason the counterfeit plagues probably stopped after the first two.

Furthermore, if the magicians did miraculously produce snakes and frogs, then what this means is that they have the power or the ability to tap into a power, to *create* life. (From a Judeo-Christian perspective, only God has that power. There is no evidence that Satan was given this power.) Neither are there any other examples in the Scripture or verifiable examples of this in recorded history. And given the technology of the day, there is no evidence that the magicians produced test-tube frogs and snakes.

It might be suggested that perhaps Moses and Aaron were merely doing the same tricks as the magicians. However, it's one thing to change a staff into a snake, but it's another to separate a body of water, the Red Sea (today called the Gulf of Suez) and then have it come back together again just as an attacking army is ready to engulf you. The water not only separated, but the ground dried so that an enormous multitude of Israelites safely passed through with their loaded carts and animals.

Now it's not a life or death issue if the magicians in Pharaoh's court used real powers or trickery to duplicate Moses' miracles, but this account is important because it is only one of two cases in the Old Testament where they actually do *something* successfully. The only other account, found in 1 Samuel 28, is the story where the medium of Endor appears to call the prophet Samuel back from the dead. (I plan to publish a full examination of this account and why I conclude it is also a bogus demonstration of powers in a sequel to this book.)

In every other account in the Old Testament the magicians, enchanters, sorcerers and the like failed miserably when they attempted to display their powers, and as a result they were mocked. Let's look at the example found in the book of Daniel.

The Babylonian Ḥakāmîm

Daniel lived around 605 B.C. When a boy, he was taken into exile by the Babylonians when Jerusalem was ransacked by Nebuchadnezzar. Being exceedingly bright, Daniel was sterilized and then made to study with Nebuchadnezzar's *ḥakāmîm* or wise men. The reason for the sterilization was so that he could potentially rise into a position of importance, minus the threat of having any heirs. This enabled ancient empires to benefit from the brightest minds of the conquered people and not be concerned with sons gaining positions of power and under-mining the regime.

The "wise men" were comprised of: magicians—*ḥarṭûmmîm;* sorcer-ers—*mᵉkashpîm* (those who whisper and cast spells); enchanters—*'ashapîm* (astrologers who cast spells); and astrologers—*kashdîm.* The *kashdîm* were called Chaldeans and studied a number-mystery lan-guage. Usually these people also studied primitive forms of astronomy, chemistry, philosophy, and other disciplines, hence the reference to the group as "wise men," which is how they were esteemed by the com-moner. Their intellectual knowledge alone was astounding to those who were not educated and virtually incontestable when combined with the practice of pretended supernatural abilities.

It was with this group that Daniel studied. And yet Daniel was a man of principle, as demonstrated by his refusal to eat the "unclean" royal food and thereby be defiled.

About a year later Nebuchadnezzar summoned all the magicians, en-chanters, sorcerers and astrologers to interpret a dream that troubled him, which is detailed in the second chapter of Daniel. His command to the wise men was to put up or shut up. Either they were to tell him the details of his dream and its interpretation, or they would be exe-cuted. Their plea to Nebuchadnezzar is humorous. "O king, live forever! Tell your servants the dream, and we will interpret it" (Dan 2:4). He refused.

They pleaded again and he responded: "I am certain that you are trying to gain time, because you realize that this is what I have firmly decided: If you do not tell me the dream, there is just one penalty for you. You have conspired to tell me misleading and wicked things, hop-ing the situation will change. So then, tell me the dream, and I will know that you can interpret it for me" (Dan 2:8-9).

When they honestly stated that this was impossible, a decree was sent out to find all the "wise men," including Daniel and his friends, in order that they might be put to death too. The end of the story is that Daniel asked for time from the king, and spent time in prayer before God, who revealed the mystery to Daniel in a vision. Daniel then described for the king his dream and gave its interpretation. Daniel was then made the head of all the *hakāmím* or wise men.

Some important points are to be gleaned from this story. First, because Daniel was a man of uncompromising principle, it logically follows that he would not engage in calling upon occult supernatural powers which were contrary to what he believed and a violation of Mosaic Law. If in his study with the "wise men" Daniel was told to use actual demonic, supernatural powers, it's a sure bet that he would have rather died than compromise his faith. Later in his life he was thrown in the lions' den for not bowing down to King Darius. He exercised his faith and refused to obey an edict requiring all subjects of the king to bow before him. For his staunch stand he was thrown in a den of lions to be eaten, from which he was miraculously spared.

Second, one can be certain that while he studied the legitimate academic pursuits of the "wise men," he discarded the rest when he realized the folly of their pretended powers. In contrast, the pagan astrologers *failed* to do anything except to attempt to con the king, who wasn't fooled.

In light of the Old Testament accounts, I am not convinced that this group ever demonstrated real supernatural powers. From the Daniel account, it appears that the only power they did try to demonstrate—although unsuccessfully—was the power of persuasion.

An Old Testament Glossary

What follows is a list of many of the Hebrew words and their meanings that are used to define these bogus workers of wonders. Accompanying each are additional comments, and references where they are mentioned.[1]

Magician (ḥarṭōm): "one who draws circles," referring to a horoscopist or astrologer; comes from the word *ḥereṭ* which means "engraver," thus one who writes or engraves and is qualified to be classified with the wise men; Daniel 2 and Exodus 7.

Sorcerer (ḵashāp): "one who whispers spells"; compared to adulterers, perjurers and those who defraud laborers in Malachi 3:5—in other words, those who are cheats and frauds; called liars in Jeremiah 27:10 and Isaiah 57:3-4; in Isaiah 47:9, 12 and 14 it is stated that their attempts will fail; sometimes translated "witch" or "witchcraft."

Astrologer ('ashāp): similar to a sorcerer and is one who practices enchantments; derived from a word that means "to lisp"—both have the same root word *sha'p;* Daniel 2.

Chaldean (kashday): professional astrologer; skilled in interpretation and schooled in mathematics, astronomy and so forth; Daniel 2.

Wise men (ḥakāmîm): Chaldean word that had a wide range of meanings from wise men to those who were cunning and crafty and subtle (possibly shifty?); in Isaiah 5:21 they are called "clever in their own sight"; in Isaiah 19:11 they give "senseless advice."

Wizard or spiritist (yidd'ōnî): "one who pretends to have great knowledge"; Isaiah 8:19 asks, why consult the *yidd'ōnîm* who "whisper and mutter"?

Secret arts or enchantments (lahaṭ): this words means "secrecy" or "mystery"; Exodus 7. Derived from the word *loṭ* which means to wrap or envelop—in other words, those who watched were ensnared in secret practices; this word does not suggest that real supernatural powers are used, rather it is reminiscent of modern-day gurus who teach their followers "the secret ways," yet never demonstrate real supernatural powers.

Soothsayer (gāzraya'): "one who determines and decides"; Daniel 2.

Sorcerer or soothsayer ('ānan): "to act covertly, to cloud over and practice magic"; Daniel 2 and Micah 5:12.

Enchantments (naḥash): another word with similar connotation as tayhem; means "to whisper, hiss, divine and learn by experience."

Charmer (ḥober): "one who ties magical knots"—a snake charmer; Psalm 58:5.

Enchanter or charmer (laḥash): "one who whispers or mumbles spells and incantations"; for instance, Psalm 58:2-5 says, "In your heart

you devise injustice, and your hands mete out violence on the earth.
Even from birth the wicked go astray; from the womb they are wayward
and speak lies. Their venom is like the venom of a snake, like that of
a cobra that has stopped its ears, that will not heed the tune of the
charmer, however skillful the enchanter may be."

Medium ('ob): in the King James Version this word is translated "one
that hath a familiar spirit"; the Hebrew word *'ob* means "one who speaks
as if from the belly"; it is derived from another word meaning "a hollow
sounding gourd"; the reason for the selection of this Hebrew word is
because the medium is a ventriloquist and does not actually contact the
spirits of the dead, but merely mimics their appearance; it was not a
popular belief at the time of the writing of the text that the spirits of
the deceased could be contacted (see I Samuel 28).

Witchcraft (qesem): derived from *qāsam* which means "to determine
by lot or magical scroll"; 1 Samuel 15:23 ("divination" in NIV).

Never Granted Authenticity
In summary, not only do these shaman-types never succeed in doing
anything that is unmistakably supernatural, they are consistently called
cheats, frauds and liars and told that their "powers" will fail. They are
scorned by the prophets for their fakery and *not* for manifesting supernatural powers. Even the very essence of the words used to define their
activity and their root derivations do not point to the fact that they have
powers. The whole group can be characterized as whisperers and moan-
ers of spells pretending to have powers, with a mix of astrology, trickery
and lies. As we will see, the New Testament records this same consistency of fraud and deception.

Chapter 13

New Testament Perspectives

THERE ARE TWO EXAMPLES IN THE NEW TESTAMENT OF MAGICIANS WHO tried to deceive those around them. The first is Simon the Sorcerer and the second is Elymas the Magician.

Simon the Sorcerer

In the wake of persecution following Pentecost, many of the new believers were forced to flee to Judea and Samaria (Acts 8:1), thus the gospel was carried to others who might not have heard. It is an example of double-jeopardy. The persecution was designed to destroy the church. Yet the very fact of persecution led to others hearing the gospel, while at the same time firming up the substantive faith of the new believers.

In Acts 8:9-24 we are told that Simon the Sorcerer amazed the folks in Samaria, which is north of Jerusalem. They boasted that he was the "Great Power." What follows is his encounter with the apostle Philip.

Now for some time a man named Simon had practiced sorcery in the city and amazed all the people of Samaria. He boasted that he was someone great, and all the people, both high and low, gave him their attention and exclaimed, "This man is the divine power known as the Great Power." They followed him because he had amazed them for a long time with his magic. But when they believed Philip as he preached the good news of the kingdom of God and the name of Jesus Christ, they were baptized, both men and women. Simon himself believed and was baptized. And he followed Philip everywhere, astonished by the great signs and miracles he saw.

When the apostles in Jerusalem heard that Samaria had accepted the word of God, they sent Peter and John to them. When they arrived, they prayed for them that they might receive the Holy Spirit, because the Holy Spirit had not yet come upon any of them; they had simply been baptized into the name of the Lord Jesus. Then Peter and John placed their hands on them, and they received the Holy Spirit.

When Simon saw that the Spirit was given at the laying on of the apostles' hands, he offered them money and said, "Give me also this ability so that everyone on whom I lay my hands may receive the Holy Spirit."

Peter answered: "May your money perish with you, because you thought you could buy the gift of God with money! You have no part or share in this ministry, because your heart is not right before God. Repent of this wickedness and pray to the Lord. Perhaps he will forgive you for having such a thought in your heart. For I see that you are full of bitterness and captive to sin."

Then Simon answered, "Pray to the Lord for me so that nothing you have said may happen to me."

To find out who Simon was and what he did or didn't do, we have to start with the Greek word which is translated "sorcery." It is the word *mageuō* which is derived from the word *magos* and literally referred to an Oriental scientist, a wise man, reminiscent of the Old Testament wise men—the *ḥakāmîm*. *Magos* is the same word used to describe the three wise men or *magi* who traveled from the East to honor the birth of Christ. *Magos* also has its roots in the Hebrew word *rab-māg* which referred to a Babylonian official. Does this mean the magi who visited Christ were occultists? Hardly.

The ancient Eastern wise men were similar to the wise men described in the passage in Daniel. They studied legitimate academic pursuits like mathematics and astronomy. Some metaphysical and cultic studies were mixed in to give their skills the appearance of real powers, or at least the ability to tap into real powers. So the reference to wise men could be to a learned person, a learned person who also studied the occult, or a not-so-learned person who studied the occult. The Magi, like Daniel, merely took in the legitimate studies and discarded the rest. But to the common person, even without their mystical studies, the *magos* would have a quasi-mystical appeal because of their studies. (For a modern-day parallel between the magos and the current study of quantum physics, read the discussion in this footnote at the end of the text.)[1]

Simon the Sorcerer revered the adulation heaped on him. He was a huckster always on the lookout for a better deal. The King James Version states that he "bewitched them with sorceries." If the translation is accurate, this could imply that he used real supernatural powers on the people of Samaria. The New International Version, however, doesn't render the translation "bewitched," but rather "amazed" (v. 11).

The Greek word in question is *existēmi,* which means "to astound or amaze." This then takes on a radically different meaning. *Existēmi* is also used to describe Simon's *reaction* to Philip (v. 13). Philip didn't "bewitch" Simon to get him to believe. Simon was merely amazed at Philip's miracles which he couldn't understand. When Simon "believed and was baptized," Philip did not cast a demon out of him. Why? Because he never really had a supernatural power. Simon's powers were merely perverted illusions cultivated for fame and fortune.

Verse 18 records that Simon later offered money to buy the ability of laying hands on people in order that they might receive the Holy Spirit. Following Philip's lead, Peter doesn't cast a demon out of Simon, but rather gives him a strong rebuke.

Now, let's look at the only other passage in the New Testament where a sorcerer claimed to have supernatural powers.

Elymas the Sorcerer

On Paul's first missionary journey the first opposition he encountered was not from supernatural powers but, like Philip, from a person pretending to have powers. Acts 13:4-12 says:

> The two of them, sent on their way by the Holy Spirit, went down to Seleucia and sailed from there to Cyprus. When they arrived at Salamis, they proclaimed the word of God in the Jewish synagogues. John was with them as their helper.
>
> They traveled through the whole island until they came to Paphos. There they met a Jewish sorcerer and false prophet named Bar-Jesus, who was an attendant of the proconsul, Sergius Paulus. The proconsul, an intelligent man, sent for Barnabas and Saul because he wanted to hear the word of God. But Elymas the sorcerer (for that is what his name means) opposed them and tried to turn the proconsul from the faith. Then Saul, who was also called Paul, filled with the Holy Spirit, looked straight at Elymas and said, "You are a child of the devil and an enemy of everything that is right! You are full of all kinds of deceit and trickery. Will you never stop perverting the right ways of the Lord? Now the hand of the Lord is against you. You are going to be blind, and for a time you will be unable to see the light of the sun."
>
> Immediately mist and darkness came over him, and he groped about, seeking someone to lead him by the hand. When the proconsul saw what had happened, he believed, for he was amazed at the teaching about the Lord.

This is a lucid account where Paul declared that Elymas created the illusion of power with trickery and deceit and not with supernatural powers. The word *magos* is translated again in this passage to describe Elymas as a sorcerer. Paul also called him a false prophet, not one who could really predict the future.[2] (See notes for a discussion of the case in Acts 16:16-18 of the woman with the spirit of divination.)

A Christian who believes that Satan does exist and possesses powers may ask, "Are you saying there are no supernatural manifestations that are evil?"

The answer is no, as I believe Satan and his powers are real, as will be detailed later. But as a journalist who covers many cases a year where Satan's supernatural powers are alleged to be at work, what I find in most cases is deliberate self-deception, misreporting and reports from those who are deluded. My personal perspective is that the two New Testament passages about Simon and Elymas provide keen insight into the nature of the battle Satan chooses to wage against the church: the preference of the use of deception rather than the overt use of supernatural powers.

When the gospel was spread outside of Jerusalem as a result of persecution, and when Paul went out on his first missionary journey, Satan attempted to deceive and confront the apostles with lies, trickery and deceit—not with supernatural powers. This is because his very nature is to lie. He wants to remain concealed. He doesn't want to be identified.

Notice that in both examples men gave credit to human flesh and blood and not to Satan for the pretended powers. Satan doesn't want to be identified as the culprit, preferring to work covertly. This is not surprising although for centuries many have assumed that these passages referred to those manifesting supernatural Satanic powers. Satan would always rather deceive with a lie than a real power.

The Father of Lies
If one is asked, "What was Satan's first act of deception?" most will point to the Garden of Eden where Eve was conned into eating the fruit from

the tree of the knowledge of good and evil. But the first deception actually took place when Satan conned himself into believing that he could be like God. He didn't deceive himself with supernatural powers. He deceived himself with a lie. This is the reason Jesus called him the "father of lies" in John 8:44: "He was a murderer from the beginning, not holding to the truth, for there is no truth in him. When he lies, he speaks his native language, for he is a liar and the father of lies."

The second act of deception which we are aware of is when Satan, with a lie, conned a large portion of the angels to rebel with him. The third act of deception, which was against the human race, was again pulled off by a lie, Genesis 3:1-5.

Now the serpent was more crafty than any of the wild animals the LORD God had made. He said to the woman, "Did God really say, 'You must not eat from any tree in the garden'?"

The woman said to the serpent, "We may eat fruit from the trees in the garden, but God did say, 'You must not eat fruit from the tree that is in the middle of the garden, and you must not touch it, or you will die.' "

"You will not surely die," the serpent said to the woman. "For God knows that when you eat of it your eyes will be opened, and you will be like God, knowing good and evil."

Satan is described as being "crafty" (v. 1). The Hebrew word for crafty is *'arûm,* which also means "one who is stripped of one's outer clothing or garment," designating rank. The same root word is used to describe Adam and Eve as naked in Genesis 2:25. The use of this word is a simple parable that tells us that Adam and Eve, in their perfect state, didn't need clothing for rank or covering, while Satan was stripped of his.

I once asked my daughter Carrie, when she was five, why Adam and Eve didn't know that they were naked in the Garden of Eden. Her wide-eyed response gave me something to think about.

"They didn't need clothes," she said, "because God was their clothing."

Satan's cloak, however, is one of illusion, where the motive, method and consequence is rooted in evil. If the evil we see in the world is a result of his constant efforts, then we should not be surprised—when it comes to claims of power—that he would try to deceive us with that which only appears to be a real power but isn't.

Counterfeit Miracles

Some theologians believe that 2 Thessalonians 2:9-10 foretells the nature of the battle Satan will wage as the lawless one, believed to be the Antichrist, comes on the world scene: "The coming of the lawless one will be in accordance with the work of Satan displayed in all kinds of counterfeit miracles, signs and wonders, and in every sort of evil that deceives those who are perishing. They perish because they refused to love the truth and so be saved."

Notice that it says, "counterfeit miracles, signs and wonder," and not real supernatural powers. Why? Because it is far more difficult to deal with a lie than to cast out an entity that is powerless against the authority of Christ.

Again, please don't misunderstand me, I am *not* saying that I don't believe in actual evil supernatural powers. My personal belief expressed by faith (as there is no camera which can photograph demons) is that they do exist. I have been in the process of documenting cases where even those who are not inclined to believe this is possible will be challenged to explain what is behind certain manifestations. But experience dictates that most of what is reported are not real supernatural powers, but that which only has the appearance of power.

In March of 1986 I attended a conference held in Berkeley on the question of Satanism and neo-paganism. It was sponsored by the Spiritual Counterfeits Project (SCP), also of Berkeley. SCP is one of the most reliable think-tanks engaged in research on different types of deceptions. SCP is often called upon by reporters and law enforcement officers when a reliable source of information is needed. They also have a hotline to give assistance to those with questions or problems with cults and new religions.

At the conference, which was attended by a broad mix of profession-als, a fairly unified perspective emerged. Of those who believed that they had participated in an actual exorcism—including the president of a college, a police officer and a noted professor of psychology—all were unanimous about two points. First, demon possession is extremely rare in *Western* culture. And second, none had ever witnessed any supernat-ural manifestations, such as levitation, during the deliverance process. In fact, most said the entity tries to hide and not be identified. The consensus was that this is because the entity knows that it can be cast out by the authority of Christ.

In addition, when the exorcism is completed, the one delivered does not run to a cult or Satanic group but in most cases to God who freed the person. This doesn't mean that Satanic forces can't operate super-naturally, but rather that Satan runs the risk of scaring people to God when he does, which is counterproductive to his deceptive goal.

Research and preparations are under way for another project that will examine the full spectrum of supernatural demonic activity and how it differs from schizophrenia, multiple-personality disorders, and other disorders.[3]

What is important for us to realize is that we do not have to be afraid of deception regardless of whether it is a supernatural power or not. The case made in the Old and New Testaments is that those who claim to have supernatural powers usually do not really have powers. Satan pre-fers to work with lies, counterfeit miracles and stratagems that place the focus of attention on man, like the examples of Simon and Elymas.

If someone is truly possessed—which should be the last option con-sidered, as it is rare in Western culture—the entity has no power over a Christian who fasts, prays for the deliverance and has compassion for the one possessed. This is my personal opinion from having examined many cases. Those at the SCP conference made that same observation, as does Mark 9:26-29.

The spirit shrieked, convulsed him violently and came out. The boy looked so much like a corpse that many said, "He's dead." But Jesus took him by the hand and lifted him to his feet, and he stood up.

After Jesus had gone indoors, his disciples asked him privately, "Why couldn't we drive it out?"

He replied, "This kind can come out only by prayer." [Some manuscripts say, "by prayer and fasting."]

If the majority of what we see and hear are counterfeit claims of power, then common sense requires us to spend the larger portion of our time on understanding how *not* to be tricked and deceived, rather than how to cast out demons. There are cases where well-meaning laity tried to cast a demon out of someone who was schizophrenic or had a multiple-personality disorder—the experience worsening the afflicted person's condition and making it more difficult to effect successful treatment.

In the Hydrick case, Mike's brother Rob, a seminary student, thought Hydrick had supernatural powers given to him by Satan; thus, he was unable to help his own brother.

Discerning between What's Real and What's False

One seminary professor, with whom I had a lengthy discussion, was disturbed with my perspective concerning the magicians and sorcerers in the New Testament. When I pointed out that Paul accused Elymas of using trickery and deceit and not supernatural powers, he said, "As soon as you start disproving the supernatural, you are leaving the door open to disproving all of the supernatural."

He was afraid I was opening a Pandora's box where nonbelievers might discredit any possibility of the supernatural and consequently reject the Christian faith.

If there is a real supernatural realm, and I believe there is, it shouldn't have to be confused with that which merely looks like it is supernatural. It should be able to stand on its own. When we knowingly or unknowingly attribute something to a supernatural power that isn't from that source, then we are participating in another form of deception.

For this reason the focus of this book is on that which appears to be a power and isn't. It is in this area that the least amount of reliable information is available. Very few of us will ever be confronted with real, evil supernatural powers, as during the times of the apostles; but all of us see and hear on the news about those who supposedly have psychic and supernatural powers.

Dr. Norm Geisler, a professor in systematic theology, states, "Fortunately the trend is reversing. There is now a heightened awareness in evangelical seminaries that deceptions, which appear to be supernatural and aren't, must be taught as a part of the total curriculum. Unless we do, those we are educating to be spiritually discerning will be crippled when they face real-life situations."[4]

As a Christian, I believe that Satan does have supernatural powers, but that he is also the "father of lies." As a journalist, I won't report something to be supernatural unless I have first run it through the mill of all the other possible options. To date, I have encountered a minute number of cases where I believed real occultic supernatural powers were operative—like possession. I have not seen any cases like those referenced in chapter 13 of the Book of Revelation, which the Scriptures state will one day occur. I am not saying that it's not possible for occultic supernatural powers to visibly manifest themselves with miraculous demonstrations; rather, after fifteen years of running down cases, I'm saying I haven't documented such an event.

There are isolated cases of demonic possession being reported today by those who are medically qualified to know the difference between it and other medical psychoses and illnesses. However, I can't film the entity that is alleged to be inside a person. What we can say is that what is happening cannot be assigned a medical or psychological explanation.

To believe that a demon is inside the person wreaking havoc requires faith; but it can't be blind faith as articulated earlier. If the manifestations only stop when the name of Christ is called upon, and there is no regression of the former behavior, then a measure of substance exists upon which to base one's faith in the belief that demon possession is real—and not misidentified or imagined. The issue here is discernment.

If you do not have a faith that allows you to believe in demons and the plausibility of Satanic powers, I would advise against developing a morbid fascination to find out. It's not worth the time and can be emotionally destructive. Even after I embraced the Christian faith, I didn't believe it was true until a number of years later when I investigated several cases. I have framed my remarks related to this issue in a biblical context because this is what I have found has been of the greatest benefit to others.

When examining claims of sorcerers, wizards and the like, we simply have to determine if they perform anything that is supernatural in the first place. The prophets in the Bible were not easily duped by their claims and were scathingly critical of the folly of their deceptions.

Isaiah the prophet, who penned more prophecies concerning the coming of the Messiah than any other Old Testament prophet, also wrote more about fraudulent claims of powers than any other Old Testament prophet. Consider some of his writings:

They are full of superstitions from the East; they practice divination like the Philistines (Is 2:6).

When men tell you to consult mediums and spiritists, who whisper and mutter, should not a people inquire of their God? (Is 8:19).

They say to the seers, "See no more visions!" and to the prophets, "Give us no more visions of what is right! Tell us pleasant things, prophesy illusions" (Is 30:10).

The prophet Jeremiah echoes the same warnings: "My hand will be against the prophets who see false visions and utter lying divinations" (Ezek 13:9).

Nowhere do we find the prophets or apostles accusing the magicians or sorcerers of having supernatural powers. What we find is that they accuse them of fraud and deceit, the effect of which is evil; and from their perspective, it is no less evil than someone who is possessed because the author is the same.

Part V
The Resurrection:
An Examination

Chapter 14

An Investigative Journalist Seeks Some Answers

HOW DOES DEVELOPING DISCERNMENT OF PSYCHIC PHENOMENA AND CLAIMS of miraculous powers apply to religious faith, the ability to believe? As the reporter who was quoted at the beginning of this book asked me, "Can't you believe something just by faith?"

A lot of people "believe" . . . even atheists who "believe" there is no God. What is often absent is a willingness to take a good hard look at what one does or doesn't believe. When we blindly hang on to our beliefs simply to protect our own agenda, truth is curbed. But a true and lasting faith is strengthened by the ability to honestly discern truth from error.

History abounds with counterfeit resurrection stories and miracle workers and each generation must reckon with its own myths. Consider the following account:

> In the first century of the Common Era, there appeared at the eastern end of the Mediterranean a remarkable religious leader who taught the worship of one true God and declared that religion meant not the sacrifice of animals, but the practice of charity and piety and the shunning of hatred and enmity. He was said to have worked miracles of goodness, casting out demons, healing the sick, raising a girl from the dead. His life of exemplary piety led some of his followers to claim that he was the son of God, though he called himself the son of a man. Accused of sedition against Rome, he was arrested. After his death, some of his followers claimed that he had risen from the dead, had appeared to them to prove that he yet lived, and then ascended to heaven.[1]

Randel Helms, associate professor of biblical literature at Arizona State University, in an article on fictitious resurrection stories, points out that this is not an account about Jesus of Nazareth, as one might assume, but of Apollonius of Tyana from Philostratus' *Life of Apollonius.* Apollonius, a faker, died about A.D. 98.

How Can We Know?

How can one determine that Jesus was any different from someone like Apollonius, who also claimed to be the divine one? The Gospels state that Jesus died, came back to life and ascended up to heaven a number of days later. Since the Scriptures are the primary source of information concerning this miracle, as a journalist in search of the facts, I wanted to know how accurate and trustworthy those accounts were. Every year I hear of reports of freewheeling all-purpose saviors who do "miracles" and claim they are the way to eternal bliss. None of these accounts check out when the facts are examined.

If the documents that report the resurrection of Christ hold up under scrutiny as records that have been unaltered throughout the centuries, then the second level of investigation would be to explore the historical

authenticity of the *events* they report. To do this I would want to research the best possible methods of counterfeiting a resurrection given
the context of the report. After all, we may have accurate copies of what
the Gospel writers reported, but that does not tell us whether or not the
eyewitnesses were deceived.

This last gauntlet would be a final safety check to prevent false reporting—or at least provide a context for me to air my reservations and
alternative theories. If, however, the account did hold up, then the
bigger question has to be addressed: why believe that it was God who
brought him back to life? Why not consider another option, such as the
possibility that Jesus' mind attained a higher state of consciousness
which turned his physical body into something eternal?

The first two questions regarding the record and the event itself are
a matter of evidence. The "why" question is a matter of faith. As I
expressed in the interview with the reporter, I am not prepared to
exercise my faith in a matter of this importance until I have reviewed
the evidence to determine if something actually happened—in this case,
a resurrection.

In regards to the Christian faith, the resurrection is the linchpin for
the faith. Remove it and what is left is Judaism. For me, reared in the
Jewish faith, eliminate the resurrection and there is no reason for me
to personally consider the Christian faith. If the resurrection of Jesus can
be determined to be true—based upon facts that hold up under scrutiny—*then* one can consider whether or not one wants to put his or her
faith in him. As veteran news commentator Harry Reasoner said, "It is
either all falsehood, or it is the truest thing in the world. . . . And it is
such a dramatic shot toward the heart that if it is not true, for Christians,
nothing is true."

What is presented here is a result of my personal investigation of the
facts. Over the years, I have studied many texts and articles and have
attentively listened to verbal arguments pro and con regarding the authenticity of the resurrection.

In an editorial on objectivity, A. M. Rosenthal, an editor with the *New*

York Times, said, "It is a given that while nobody can achieve pristine
objectivity, every journalist can strive incessantly toward fairness."

The facts in this section are presented as fairly as possible. The conclusions, however, are obviously my own. They are to be read as if one
is reading editorial comments in a newspaper—my interpretation of
what the facts mean. I've tried not to blur the facts by my opinions. It
is still your decision whether or not this alleged miracle really happened
and why.

In this editorial context I have included this summation regarding the
resurrection of Christ so that both those who do and those who don't
embrace the Christian story will further grapple with what they believe
about the resurrection account. This is not intended as an all-inclusive
examination—as that would take volumes—but rather a fresh perspective on an age-old question.

To find out what did or didn't happen, I approached this task the
same as any other case—past or present. Here, the key questions that
need to be answered are: what really happened and why?

If I received a call in my office that a deceased thirty-three-year-old
man came back to life three days after he died, I would want to get the
answers to three questions:

1. Is the person whom the story is allegedly about a real person or
just the invention of some crazed follower?

2. Did he die?

3. Did he really come back to life in a way that defies expert medical
explanation?

Then, if the facts checked out, I would go through one more step as
a safety precaution before reporting the story.

I would consult other experts on deception from various disciplines
for their input to construct the best counterfeit resurrection scam capable of convincing several hundred mentally balanced persons that
someone had died and come back to life. I would then compare such
a scenario with the facts in the case reported. If I found that the invented
method didn't hold up, only then would I report the case for others to

consider.

Did Jesus Live?

To begin, let's start with the first question: Was there really a first-century person known as Jesus of Nazareth? And is the biblical description of him accurate?

Here is a report from an historian who was *not* a follower of Jesus and therefore not likely to have been taken in if the facts had been fabricated:

> At about this time lived Jesus, a wise man, if indeed one might call him a man. For he was one who accomplished surprising feats and was a teacher of such people as are eager for novelties. He won over many of the Jews and many of the Greeks. He was the Messiah. When Pilate, upon an indictment brought by the principal men among us, condemned him to the cross, those who had loved him from the very first did not cease to be attached to him.

This account was recorded by the Roman citizen and Jewish historian, Flavius Josephus, in his account, *The Antiquities of the Jews,* in approximately A.D. 92 or 93. How reliable was Josephus?

> An important feature of Josephus's writings is their high degree of detail, and where they can be checked from archaeology, as for instance in the case of their description of the fall of Masada, they are impressively accurate. Masada's excavation even revealed inscribed potsherds used in the casting of lots before the defenders' dramatic suicide, as Josephus described. It is also quite clear that Josephus, although certainly not a Christian, was interested in matters of religion.[2]

This observation about Josephus is offered by Ian Wilson in his book *Jesus, the Evidence,* a text critical of the claims of Christ. (While some scholars believe that the resurrection account in Josephus' writings was later added by a scribe trying to deceptively shade the historical record, the majority of scholars accept Jesus' physical place in history as a real person at the time prescribed.)

There are also other accounts about Jesus of Nazareth that exist apart from those found in Scriptures. For this reason historians and researchers, regardless of their personal beliefs about Jesus, generally accept as fact that he was a person in history. Now the next question must be answered: Did he really die?

Did He Die by Crucifixion?

If Jesus lived as a man—and it is now almost twenty centuries later— it can be assumed that he died. If he was merely a man, like you and I, he would have naturally died of old age, if not stricken by an accident or disease while younger. So the question here is, did he die by crucifixion? Josephus confirms that he was crucified, and it is unlikely that he would have invented the story since he was known for wanting to please the Romans. But the question remains, did Christ *die* by crucifixion? Or could he have somehow survived in a comatose state?

What follows are excerpts of the most current medical findings published in the *Journal of the American Medical Association* in March 1986, addressing the question of Jesus' death and the plausibility of anyone surviving this form of execution. The article was appropriately entitled, "On the Physical Death of Jesus Christ."

The rigors of Jesus' ministry (that is, traveling by foot throughout Palestine) would have precluded any major physical illness or a weak general constitution. Accordingly, it is reasonable to assume that Jesus was in good physical condition before his walk to Gethsemane [where he was arrested]. However, during the 12 hours between 9 PM Thursday and 9 AM Friday, he had suffered great emotional stress (as evidenced by hematidrosis—the condition where the capillaries burst and create a condition where one appears to "sweat" blood), abandonment by his closest friends (the disciples), and a physical beating (after the first Jewish trial). . . . These conditions may have rendered Jesus particularly vulnerable to the adverse hemodynamic (bleeding) effects of the scourging.

As the Roman soldiers repeatedly struck the victim's back with full force, the iron balls would cause deep contusions, and the leather thongs and sheep bones would cut into the skin and subcutaneous tissues. Then, as the flogging continued, the lacerations would tear into the underlying skeletal muscles and produce quivering ribbons of bleeding flesh. Pain and blood loss generally set the stage for circulatory shock. The extent of the blood loss may well have determined how long the victim would survive on the cross. . . .

The archaeological remains of a crucified body, found in an ossuary near Jerusalem and dating from the time of Christ, indicate that the nails were tapered spikes approximately 5 to 7 inches long with a square shaft 3/8 inches across.

With the arms outstretched but not taut (the prisoner is stretched out on the cross), the wrists were nailed to the patibulum (cross piece). It has been shown that the ligaments and bones of the wrist can support the weight of a body hanging from them, but the palms cannot. Accordingly, the iron spikes probably were driven between the radius and the carpals or between the two rows of carpal bones, either proximal to or through the strong bandlike flexor retinaculum and the various intercarpal ligaments. . . . Furthermore, the driven nail would crush or sever the rather large sensorimotor median nerve. The stimulated nerve would produce excruciating bolts of fiery pain in both arms.[3]

After detailing how the feet were nailed to the upright, the article continues to explain that as the prisoner hangs from the cross, the weight of the body, pulling down on the outstretched arms and shoulders, freezes the muscles attached to the rib cage in such a manner that exhaling is almost impossible. In order to exhale, the prisoner must push upward with the legs aided by the nailed wrists. The result is searing pain in the arms due to the severed nerves in the wrist, muscle cramping, and eventual asphyxiation as the prisoner tired—no longer able to push upward to exhale. In some cases the legs were broken to speed up the execution process. The prisoner, no longer able to push up and get a breath, dies in a matter of minutes.

The conclusion of the three contributing doctors was that Jesus did indeed die by crucifixion. Further research reveals that there are no written records of anyone surviving this ordeal save one poor rogue who was declared innocent and taken down before he died. So one can safely conclude that Jesus did in fact die as a result of crucifixion and did not somehow just pass out and survive in a comatose state.

There is little to dispute the fact that Jesus lived and that he died as a result of being executed by crucifixion, leaving the most important question: did he really come back to life?

Chapter 15

Accounts of the Resurrection

THE MOST COMPLETE DESCRIPTIONS WE HAVE STATING THAT JESUS CAME back to life are found in documents that are centuries old: the Gospels. Can they be trusted as reliable, first, in what they reported, and second, that they were not changed down through the centuries?

The Bible, including both the Old and New Testaments, was written over a period of sixteen hundred years by over forty diverse authors from kings to peasants. It was penned on three continents in three different languages. The first section, the Old Testament, is made up of thirty-nine books. It begins with the creation of the world and then chronicles the history of the Hebrew people up until about 444 B.C. The second section, the New Testament, is comprised of twenty-seven books that chronicle the life and teachings of Jesus as well as a short history of the beginnings of the early church.

Written over such a lengthy span of time from numerous cultural settings, it is extraordinary that there is the same consistent theme throughout the Bible: God's plan to redeem our imperfect world. The first to believe that the resurrection story was true were Jews and other people from countries around the Mediterranean Sea.

Documentary Evidence

Accounts of the resurrection are found in the New Testament in what are called the four Gospels, which means "good news." These four short books are commonly referred to by the names of their authors—Matthew, Mark, Luke and John. Matthew and John were two of Jesus' twelve apostles. They were eyewitnesses of the events recorded. Mark and Luke, although not eyewitnesses, relied upon eyewitnesses for their accounts. Scholars are divided over whether Matthew and John actually wrote the accounts which bear their name, though there is more acceptance that the apostle John is the likely author of the Gospel of John. Each account records the resurrection story from the slightly different perspectives of separate authors. Therefore, one must read all four accounts for the best overall view.

These four books were originally written on papyrus made from the papyrus plant, a reed found in shallow lakes in Egypt and Syria. Very few manuscripts of any kind written on papyrus have survived to the present unless they were buried in containers in the dry Egyptian desert or in caves similar to the ones at Qumran where the Dead Sea Scrolls (which included scrolls and fragments from every book in the Old Testament except Esther) were discovered in 1947 and the years following. It was therefore necessary to copy original manuscripts as they deteriorated, so the texts could continue to be used.

The first-century Christians expected Christ's imminent return (within a few years) to the earth to set up his kingdom as he had promised. The effort and cost of copying the Gospels on another type of material such as leather or parchment (which would endure over several centuries) was not perceived as a vital need. The cost of recording just one of the Gospels on parchment would have been the equivalent of thirty goats— a small fortune by first-century standards. In addition, most of the new Christian converts were not Jewish and not literate. Thus an abundance of scrolls were unnecessary.

As a result, we have no original documents, only early copies. But that's not unusual for ancient writings. The *Iliad* by Homer, for example, was written around 900 B.C., but we have no surviving manuscripts dating from before about 400 B.C.—five hundred years later. In contrast, the earliest fragment from the New Testament (which was completed by A.D. 100) is called the *John Ryland Manuscript* and dates around A.D. 130. A number of others follow at later dates starting with the *Chester Beatty Papyri* (A.D. 200). Two complete manuscripts—the *Codex Vaticanus* (A.D. 325) and *Codex Sinaiticus* (A.D. 350)—date within two hundred and fifty years of the completion of the New Testament.

Compared to the *Iliad,* our earliest copies had much less time for errors to have been included in the copying. University speaker Josh McDowell points out that "we are able to document 24,633 manuscripts and portions . . . in Greek and other early versions of the New Testament."[1] In comparison, 643 copies or fragments are available for the *Iliad.*

McDowell further points out that, "as a result of research done at the British Museum, we are now able to document 89,000 quotations from the New Testament in early church writings [extra-biblical sources]. If you destroyed all the Bibles and Biblical manuscripts, one could reconstruct all but 11 verses of the entire New Testament from quotations found in other materials written within 150 to 200 years after the time of Jesus Christ!"[2]

Scholars determine the credibility of these manuscripts by many disciplines including: accuracy of the historical events recorded in the light of modern archaeological finds; how the accounts fair against other records of the same time period; and the soundness and consistency of the record. In the case of the Gospels, the question is: are they consistent or do they appear to be the rantings of deranged followers? Most scholars will concede that the Gospels are a record of what their authors believed to be true and not the writings of mad men. And in respect to the historical information recorded, they have been found reliable.

But simply because the authors appear to have had lucid minds and could accurately record historical events—as corroborated by historical and archaeological finds—doesn't mean the resurrection actually happened, that the authors were not each deceived. Numerous reporters today have been deceived by current miracle workers, even though there is a broader network of information available to rule out possible deceptions.

Only the Resurrection
A student on a campus once asked me if any of the other miracles in the Bible can be examined in detail like the resurrection. From my perspective as an investigator and journalist, the answer is no. The resurrection is the only miracle where there is enough physical and circumstantial evidence to make a concrete determination and avoid acceptance solely reliant upon faith.

It is impossible, for example, to reconstruct the splitting of the Red Sea or any of the other great miracles recorded in the Old or New Testament. A case in point is Christ's first miracle, the changing of water into wine at a wedding ceremony as recorded in John 2. Taken by itself, it is reminiscent of an old magician's trick.

Around the turn of the century, Think-a-Drink Hoffman, a noted stage magician, became famous for an offbeat trick. Holding a clear glass pitcher of water, he would invite anyone in the audience to name any drink: lemonade, bourbon, a mixed drink—any drink at all. Lined up in front of him were a row of clear cut-crystal glasses. Picking up one of the glasses, he would pour the clear water into the glass and it would visually change to the selected drink. He would then offer the glass to the spectator. Color, smell, flavor and even the strength of the drink matched the spectator's expectations. It was a truly amazing trick.

If someone had tried to convince me to embrace the Christian faith based on the miracle of Jesus changing water into wine, I probably would have replied, "If you think that's something, you should have seen Think-a-Drink Hoffman!"

Today, even though by faith I believe this miracle of Jesus' was authentic and not a trick, I can't prove it. I can't prove that Jesus didn't do the same thing as Think-a-Drink Hoffman. There just aren't enough facts surrounding the Gospel account of this miracle to verify this to someone who wants proof. I believe that this is true of every one of Christ's miracles except the resurrection. There are no other records—apart from the Bible—that specifically confirm in detail his other miracles.

It is the resurrection account, though, that sets Jesus apart from other perceived religious leaders like Muhammad, Buddha and Confucius. None of the latter is reported to have miraculously come back to life. It is for this reason that Christianity is the only major religion of the world that stands or falls on an alleged historical event—the resurrection.

Many nonmiraculous theories have been suggested regarding what actually took place. In one theory, Jesus is believed to have hypnotized his disciples and by a posthypnotic trance, convinced them that he came back to life. In other words, they only *imagined* that they saw him. Having questioned a number of experts on hypnosis and transinduction states, this is simply not possible. One can't hypnotize hundreds of people simultaneously to see the same vision several days or weeks later. It is just not possible.

Another theory was that Christ was drugged when he was on the cross and that he never died. This doesn't add up because of the fact that, as mentioned in the last chapter, there is no written account of anyone ever surviving crucifixion. Even if he had been drugged, the torture endured would have kept him in bed for many weeks recuperating. Who would follow a stretcher-ridden Messiah?

None of the pseudo-resurrection theories with which I am acquainted are good enough to fool people en masse. One of the cleverest I have encountered is what is used in Haiti to produce zombies—the living dead. Voodoo priests use this deception to appear to call back the dead from the grave, but with a curse.

The victim, who has had a curse placed on him, first mysteriously dies. Then, several days later, after being buried, the same person is seen alive, but minus their thinking faculties. These zombies are then used for slave labor and serve as a fearful warning of what happens to those who do not fall in line.

The secret of how this was accomplished remained a mystery until recently. Many assumed that it was a demonstration of occult supernatural powers. The real culprit, however, is the voodoo priest and an exotic powdery compound formulated with tetrodotoxin, one of the most potent nerve poisons in the world. It induces paralysis, causing respiration to drop and oxygen demand to fall so low that a victim can survive for hours on the air in a coffin. Dr. Irv Stone, the noted head of forensics for the Dallas Crime Lab, confirmed that the tetrodotoxin is so toxic that if enough merely touches the surface of one's skin, it has the capacity to put the victim in a comatose state.

The mixture of ingredients is ground into a fine powder and spread out like fine dust on a location such as a window sill, a door handle or any other likely place that the intended victim will touch with their fingers. Within hours, the victim lapses into a cataleptic state where respiration and pulse cannot be detected in primitive medical conditions.

The victim is then declared dead and buried in a casket. The conspirator, knowing from experience about how long the comatose victim can remain alive in the casket and taking into consideration the limited amount of oxygen, discreetly digs up the brain-damaged victim before death. Morbidly, the zombie is now used to inspire terror.

This method, however, while effective in instilling fear, will not produce a person healthy enough to be capable of inspiring followers.

Counterfeiting the Resurrection

After reviewing many options, I was able to formulate a method for counterfeiting a resurrection capable of deceiving intelligent and street-wise men and women. It presupposes that the perpetrator had a deviant need for recognition and adulation, even at the cost of his or her own life. This is the best method I know of that could have been used to convince Christ's followers that he came back to life after being publicly executed by crucifixion.

First, it will be presupposed that Jesus had a twin brother or someone with whom he was acquainted who looked, acted and spoke like him. This twin would have to have scars carved into his wrists and feet simulating one who has been crucified. The scars, inflicted several weeks prior to the mock resurrection, must be totally healed to convince the apostles that "Jesus" was healed.

(It is not completely out of the question to speculate that someone might do this. I know of a fakir-type who is publicly crucified as a publicity stunt for about half an hour each year. During the ghastly demonstration, nails—rather than spikes—are actually driven through his hands and feet. Of course, this is a long way from going through with one's own execution, but it does demonstrate how far some people will go for attention.)

After the scars are in place in this counterfeit scenario, Jesus would then have to cause some kind of disturbance or break a law to force his arrest and be crucified. This means that he possessed a crazed desire to die in exchange for being falsely worshiped after his death. The reason for his arrest, though, would have to be carefully thought out so that it would be consistent with his teachings. He couldn't commit a gross crime such as murder to secure a death sentence. If he did, his credibility as a loving Messiah would be disavowed and his teaching considered hypocrisy. In Roman-occupied Israel, claiming to be the Son of God would be one severe way to force the political forces to arrest him.

It was essential for Pontius Pilate, the Roman governor appointed by the emperor over this tiny country, and the local religious leaders to keep the peace. If an insurrection erupted because the people of the street followed the "son of God," Pilate might lose his post and the religious leaders their last vestige of power. With a cleverly managed "messiah" campaign that threatens the political need to maintain control, Jesus could become someone that the authorities would desire to eliminate. Assuming with proper timing that the necessary pressure is brought to bear and Jesus is crucified on the charge of stirring up riots with his claims that he is the Son of God, the body would then have be stolen to create an empty tomb and the illusion of the resurrected.

The Gospel accounts state that Jesus was buried in a rich man's tomb. Tombs were often a rock-hewn cavern in the side of a hill sealed by a large stone, estimated to be around two thousand pounds. The accounts further state that a Roman guard unit was positioned in front of the tomb at the request of the chief priests and Pharisees.

But how did the "grave robbers" get past this elite Roman guard? Josh McDowell writes,

The Justinian Code, compiled in the sixth century, mentions in Digest #49 all the offenses that required the death penalty under Roman law. The fear of their superiors' wrath and the possibility of death meant that they paid close attention to the most minute details of their job. One way a guard was put to death was by being stripped of his clothes and then burned alive with a fire started with his garments. If it was not apparent which soldier had failed in his duty, then lots were drawn to see which one would be punished with death for the guard unit's failure. Certainly the entire unit would not have fallen asleep with that kind of threat over their heads. Dr. George Currie, a student of Roman military discipline, wrote that fear of punishment "produced flawless attention to duty, especially in the night watches."[3]

The request for the guard unit was issued because, while alive, Jesus is recorded to have predicted that he would rise from the grave. None of the officials wanted his body to be stolen leaving an empty tomb to start a fanatical messianic cult. In Matthew 20:18-19, prior to his execution, Jesus said: "We are going up to Jerusalem, and the Son of Man will be betrayed to the chief priests and the teachers of the law. They will condemn him to death and will turn him over to the Gentiles to be mocked and flogged and crucified. On the third day he will be raised to life!"

To be able to empty his tomb after his death, Jesus would have had to devise a way to circumvent the crack guard unit. But first he would have had to anticipate that they would have been posted; after all, it was not standard practice nor was it requested by his followers but by the Jewish leaders.

There was only one viable option for getting into the sealed tomb: entry had to be made via a secret passage. To do this, the tomb, which is recorded as having been newly hewn, had to be prepared in advance with a secret passage similar to those constructed in the pyramids. Then, those party to the scheme could steal and dispose of the body. This means that Joseph of Arimathea, the wealthy man who is recorded to have provided the tomb, was either an accomplice or was cleverly conned into the scam.

Once the tomb is discovered empty, the "twin" had only to make his appearance, with healed scars, and announce that he was alive and was indeed the Messiah. With proper timing, this would fool many into becoming believers. There are problems, though, with even this elaborate scheme for fraud.

The Unexpected Wound
It is recorded that the attending executioner thrust a spear in Jesus' side to insure that he was dead. "The soldiers therefore came and broke the legs of the first man who had been crucified with Jesus, and then those of the other. But when they came to Jesus and found that he was already dead, they did not break his legs. Instead, one of the soldiers pierced Jesus' side with a spear, bringing a sudden flow of blood and water" (Jn 19:32-34). After his resurrection, Thomas, one of the apostles, de-

manded confirmation of that scar before he would accept the fact of
Jesus' resurrection. It was this scar that Thomas wanted to see (Jn 20:24-
25).

Traditionally, Thomas has been labeled "doubting Thomas" because
he didn't believe the apostles when they said they had seen Jesus appear
to them—apparently risen from the dead. He wasn't present when Jesus
first appeared to the apostles after his death. But Thomas certainly didn't
lack faith. The tenacity of his faith is revealed in an earlier account prior
to Jesus' death.

Then he [Jesus] said to his disciples, "Let us go back to Judea."

"But Rabbi," they said, "a short while ago the Jews tried to stone
you, and yet you are going back there?" . . .

Then Thomas (called Didymus) said to the rest of the disciples,
"Let us also go, that we may die with him" (Jn 11:7-8, 16).

Thomas was the first one willing to die for Jesus, but to believe unconfirmed reports that someone came back from the dead would be hard
for anyone to swallow. Without any facts, would you have believed the
apostles if put in Thomas's place? Now if several hundred had testified
by then that they had seen Jesus, that's one thing; but Thomas was
hearing this from those who had been distraught and under great
strain—men who had fled in fear after Jesus' arrest. Considering the
emotional trauma they had been through, perhaps Thomas thought that
they had mistakenly seen someone who only *looked* like Jesus, or even
worse—an impostor.

Jesus encouraged those who had difficulty in believing in him to
"believe on the evidence of the miracles themselves." Thomas needed
more on which to base his belief than a story offered by stressed-out
friends who only a few days before had deserted Christ.

Thomas's exercise in discernment might even be shrewder than what
we see on the surface. He may have thought that the apostles saw an
impostor with similar scars. His demand to see the scar in Christ's side
is an important detail.

No one could have predicted ahead of time that Jesus would die quickly. He died before the two thieves crucified on either side of him, thus he did not have his legs broken (Jn 19:31-37) to hasten the execution. The religious leaders pressed for a quick conclusion to the execution in order that the bodies could be removed before the Sabbath, the day of rest. By breaking the legs, as already noted, the prisoner could not push up to breathe.

Like the unit that guarded the tomb, if the executioner did not successfully carry out his task, the executioner could be put to death. This is another probable reason that there are no written accounts of someone surviving the complete process of crucifixion.

Therefore, to insure that Christ was dead, John 19:34 states that one of the soldiers thrust his spear into Christ's side; however, the spear could have been thrust anywhere the executioner wanted to insure death. It could have been thrust upward directly under the sternum into the heart or lungs, into the carotid artery in the neck, or into Christ's other side. And there are no historical records which indicate that there was a limit to the number of thrusts. So it's not difficult to imagine why Thomas wanted to see the scar in the correct location.

The only option open for perfectly duplicating the scar in a double would have been to have the executioner in on the scam, having been paid to inflict the wound in the right place. This is a real long shot, however, because if he was caught, he would have been killed. And not even Christ's most ardent followers, the apostles, were willing to die for him until *after* they saw Christ alive.

What's interesting is that the full-blown reason for Thomas's desire to see the scar in the side is never articulated in the Scriptures. If I had been trying to create a fictitious account, I would have made a big deal over why Thomas wanted to see the scar in the side. The Scriptures don't do this. They simply state that he wanted to see the scar in Christ's side. There is no mention that he wanted to be sure that the scar matched the executioner's work. It is recorded, though, that when Thomas saw Jesus and the scar in the side, he believed.

A week later his disciples were in the house again, and Thomas was with them. Though the doors were locked, Jesus came and stood among them and said, "Peace be with you!" Then he said to Thomas, "Put your finger here; see my hands. Reach out your hand and put it into my side. Stop doubting and believe."

Thomas said to him, "My Lord and my God!"

Then Jesus told him, "Because you have seen me, you have believed; blessed are those who have not seen and yet have believed" (Jn 20:26-29).

Jesus said future generations would be blessed for believing without being able to touch for themselves the scar in his side, as did Thomas. He did not expect a blind leap of faith but rather faith based upon the weight of the evidence at hand. If, as many scholars believe, the Old Testament is a constant foreshadowing of the life, death and resurrection of Jesus, and the New Testament account of his resurrection is true, then this is *the* miracle that must have concrete facts and documents for you and I to weigh in order to believe it is true.

Chapter 16

Evidence under Scrutiny

T ODAY REAL MIRACLES ARE EXTREMELY INFREQUENT AND NONE, AS OF THE writing of this book, have been captured as they happen by the lens of a camera. Maybe some day one will. What we do see and hear, however, are an extraordinary number of accounts of weeping Madonnas and the like which are never verified. In 1987 I viewed a network news broadcast where visions of the Virgin Mary were reported in Medjugorje, Yugoslavia. On camera, people pointed to what they believed were visions of Mary and crosses rotating. As these things were supposedly taking place, a camera was trained on the "miracles," yet the eye of the camera recorded nothing miraculous. In the last six years an estimated five million tourists have flooded this town to see the visions—good business, no doubt, but few if any miracles.

One of the objectives of this book is to help those who desire to express their faith in the paranormal or supernatural to do so from solid ground. In respect to the resurrection of Christ, there are two points that cannot be resolved even if there had been a camera trained on Christ's body at the very moment he arose.

First, there is no evidence conclusive enough—on its own—to prove to the generations after Christ that he was resurrected. And second, even if there were, it would not prove that he was the Son of God, brought back to life by God.

Imagine if the technology were available and video cameras had been trained on Christ's body from the time of his entombment until his resurrection. On video tape one could actually see life surge back into his body, taking on a perfect form and then being transported out of sight. No doubt some who would view the taped footage in future generations would think the videotaped record was a fake, a created relic.

The Shroud of Turin, which many believe to be Christ's burial cloth, is an example. Some believe that the imprint on the cloth, which resembles a crucified body, is the result of the transformation of his body when it was resurrected—the result of some kind of flash effect.

While the Shroud makes for interesting conversation, there is no way to know for certain that it really is Christ's burial shroud. After speaking with those who have closely examined the evidence, I personally don't believe it is the actual shroud. But even if it is, it doesn't prove anything concerning the divine nature of Christ or the nature of the resurrection. It doesn't prove *how* and *why* it happened.

The Implications of the Resurrection

To verify that something happened—that Jesus came back to life—requires tangible evidence and not blind faith. However, to accept the Christian beliefs that . . .

☐ Jesus was the Son of God;

☐ that while on the cross he absorbed the sin of the world so that when a believer dies, the evil part is removed insuring perfect unity with a perfect God;

☐ that God the Father in heaven brought him back to life and that he ascended into heaven;

☐ and that one can enter heaven upon death only by believing that Jesus was the Messiah;

. . . to accept these things as truth requires faith. There is simply no way to factually prove these beliefs which are the foundation of the Christian faith. Furthermore, it is possible for someone to accept the event of the resurrection and deny the Christian version of why it happened.

People who subscribe to what has become known as the New Age Movement might suggest that Jesus got in touch with his inner self resulting in the creation of a perfect state. Others would say that having achieved perfection after being reincarnated many times, Jesus naturally was resurrected. The "why" explanations can be endless. So where does this leave us?

After shooting the Hydrick case, I concluded that the point was not that a twenty-one-year-old psychic could fool millions of people with tricks, but rather what was recorded was a parable of what can happen when the family unit breaks down. Family breakdown often combines with the need people have to believe in *something;* and when discernment is absent, deception's door is left wide open. Many elements in that case had to be carefully examined in order to get a clear picture of not only what was going on but, more important, what it means for you and me. The resurrection of Christ must be approached the same way. What does it mean?

If Christ's resurrection took place isolated from anything that came before or after, its effect on history would have been minimal. Some would no doubt form a "religion" around the event, while most would consider it something interesting to discuss around the campfire. If the "why it happened" is not unmistakably clear, the resurrection itself would not have been enough to sustain my belief or the belief of millions of others.

Every other alleged resurrection account that I have examined comes up short on credibility. In the Appolonius account, the same text that cites his "resurrection" is the telling of how he accused an old blind beggar in Ephesus of being inhabited by a demon. Appolonius then directs the crowd to stone the blind man. At first they resist until further exhorted. After the stoning and the stones are removed, the blind beggar is gone and a corpse of a large dog is found in its place.

For me, this does not have the ring of an authentic messiah who is concerned with compassion for mankind. When Jesus was confronted with a blind man (Jn 9), he healed him; and when confronted with the demon possessed, he mercifully released the captive from torment (Mk 9:14-32). The deeds of Jesus match his teachings. They are not in opposition to one another, but are consistent.

Standing the Test of Time

The book *Holy Blood, Holy Grail* appeared on the market a few years ago. It was highly touted on all the talk shows as giving positive proof that Jesus was married, rendering the Scriptural accounts inaccurate. I immediately purchased it because the authors stated that they had credible and verifiable documents from antiquity to substantiate their claims. The book turned out to be a crude hoax. It was formatted in such a way as to lead the reader along without providing any definitive or supporting facts. The conclusions of the book were pure conjecture.

To be intellectually honest, the Christian must never be afraid to examine other resurrection stories when presented by critics. If the story of Christ's resurrection is true, it will stand the test of time. So far, it has survived almost two thousand years. Claims of other resurrections have not.

Through the ages, many have become Christians for a multitude of reasons that don't have anything to do with examining the facts of the resurrection.

Some have believed since they were young that the story of Christ is true simply because their parents and those before them have believed it to be true.

Some embrace the faith out of a sense of desperation. Divorce, an addiction, depression or hopelessness can be one of many catalysts that forces a person to come to grips with the meaning or the lack of meaning in one's life. They want to find something to believe in that has permanence and is lasting, a belief that provides an answer to the pain in his or her life, or answers the question: What happens to me when I die?

Others have come to faith through an intellectual quest for knowledge.

Then there are people, like myself, who don't fit into these categories, but who for one motivating reason or another believe the Christian story of this world in the light of all the other story-options.

Even if one's reason for embracing the faith is embedded in a positive motivation (such as a search for stability), if the resurrection story isn't true, the Christian faith is a heinous deception. What would be even more grievous is if there really is another way to get to the place called heaven. If Jesus of Nazareth was resurrected from the grave, however, then no thinking person should turn away from genuinely considering what this means.

In this brief look I have tried to summarize some of the highlights of what I have found concerning Christ in contrast with other cases I have examined. Although I believe that the resurrection was an actual, historical event and that the Christian story of why it happened is true, that does not give me or anyone else the right to coerce someone else to accept this belief. Christ never forced anyone to believe in him. Neither did the apostles. It must be a decision born of a mind that comes to its own conclusions and a heart that can ponder without illusions. If the story of the resurrection and what it means is true, then it needs no props to hold it up when contrasted with all the other stories we are asked to consider.

To say that God came to earth in the form of a man to pay the price for our evil is an extraordinary thought. If there really is a God, one would expect that he would make every attempt to communicate this to us in every way possible short of violating our free will. What follows is the rest of Harry Reasoner's reflection on this in a Christmas editorial on December 23, 1979, on "60 Minutes."

It's a startling idea, of course. My guess is that the whole story—that a virgin was selected by God to bear his Son as a way of showing his love and concern for man—it's my guess that in spite of all the lip service they have given it, it is not an idea that has been popular with theologians. It's a somewhat illogical idea, and theologians love logic almost as much as they love God. It's so revolutionary a thought that it probably could only come from a God who is beyond logic and beyond theology. It has a magnificent appeal. Almost nobody has seen God and almost nobody has any real idea of what He's like; and the truth is that among men the idea of seeing God suddenly and standing in the very bright light is not necessarily a completely comfortable and appealing idea.

But everybody has seen babies, and most people like them. If God wanted to be loved as well as feared, He moved correctly here. If He wanted to know His people, as well as rule them, He moved correctly here, for a baby growing up learns all about people. If God wanted to be intimately a part of man, He moved correctly, for the experience of birth and familyhood is our most intimate and precious experience.

So it came beyond logic. It is either all falsehood, or it is the truest thing in the world. It is a story of the great innocence of God the baby, God in the power of man; and it is such a dramatic shot toward the heart, that if it is not true, for Christians nothing is true. So, if a Christian is touched only once a year, the touching is still worth it. And maybe on some given Christmas . . . the touch will take.

The Nature of Faith
Faith as defined in Hebrews 11:1 is: (1) knowing what you hope for and

(2) being certain of what you cannot see. For me, I know what I hope for: I am sure that Christ will fulfill his promise and one day receive me in heaven. And my certainty has come about because I have weighed the evidence of his resurrection, and I have found it to be factually convincing.

It wasn't planned, but this chapter was appropriately written during the week prior to Easter. Each year my church reenacts the final days of Christ leading up to his resurrection. This year's production drew over ten thousand people. I observed the emotional impact of this story on people from many walks of life and nationalities: a Chinese family freed from the Cultural Revolution, newly widowed mothers, those who stride with pomp and circumstance, a hand-clasped couple anxiously awaiting marriage, construction workers at rest and an elderly man pensively holding his grandson. Most knew the story by heart. Some heard it for the first time. None were unmoved, even if they didn't believe. Observing this response, I thought, if this story isn't true, then God help us. And if it is, he already has.

Epilog

TODAY THERE'S NO SHORTAGE OF THOSE QUICK TO EXPLOIT PEOPLE WHO SAY they have powers. When I pointed out to the Dallas disc jockey the danger of Catchings giving advice and counsel to complete strangers, his response was one of indifference. No *credible* counselor would do that. If a news account appeared that a prominent psychiatrist or psychologist knowingly did the same thing, there would be a public outcry for regulation.

One psychic actually uses this as a rationale for his deception. He justifies his activities by complaining that many psychologists, psychiatrists, pastors and priests are manipulative, just in it for the money and give bad counsel. He purports that he is merely filling the void. This line of logic is deceptively self-serving. The fact that there are ineffective counselors doesn't give one license to traffic in deception. It's like saying because there are some doctors who have a large number of malpractice suits, we should go to a voodoo priest to be healed, rather than seeking other competent help.

I have never seen a case where a person did not become more enmeshed in a deceptive mindset once the psychic or fraudulent activity is accepted as real.

In the coming years, psychics will shed their various titles and techniques for new ones as their deceptions are exposed. Recently high-tech Japan has experienced a boom in psychic cold readings for executives through the study of blood types, if you can believe it. In this country iridology, the observation of the characteristics of the iris, is in vogue and is used as a catalyst for cold readings. But the principles by which psychics operate will remain the same, as they have for centuries. And in order to continue to captivate the buyer, their claims of power will become more exotic.

Channeling, a New Age Wave

The next new wave that is gaining momentum is called "channeling." Channelers claim that they can mentally communicate with one another across long distances, contact spirits, enter into a regressive state so that one's spirit can get in touch with one's past life and even travel to far places in this ethereal state.

The training is usually a mixture of Eastern mystical jargon, positive thinking, meditation, relaxation techniques and sensitivity sessions where one learns to get in touch with one's "inner self."

Many channelers are slicker and better educated than those like Hydrick and Catchings, appealing to the professional who has money and a mind to burn.

A *New York Times* account (April 11, 1988) stated that the publisher, G. P. Putnam's Sons, resisted publishing a book on this—"until a psychic medium gave its executives 'readings' with the dead that so bowled them over they signed him to a six-figure deal."

Even more disheartening is that they are harder to disentangle from their victims. Only in rare cases is there a physical "smoking gun" to expose. If you know of someone involved with channeling, encourage them to quit. It is one of the most convoluted and insidious kinds of activity I have ever run across. And as did Hydrick, some channelers present a front that what they teach is merely another extension of Christianity—an attaining of a "Christ consciousness."

Adding to the confusion is that the current use of the term *New Age* or the *New Age movement* collectively refers to the kinds of activities seen at psychic fairs plus everything from Transcendental Meditation, Zen, unconventional corporate training seminars, extraterrestrial travels. . . . The list is endless.

Parents should find other fanciful pursuits for their kids than Dungeons and Dragons, Ouija boards and Tarot cards. We don't want to expose kids to something we'll later regret.

Testing the Powers

Testing the powers can be gritty business, but the alternative can be destructive chaos—even in matters of state and international affairs as illustrated by the Reagan's plunge into the world of astrology and psychic predictors.

When those who embrace the Christian faith toss honest discernment aside and blindly accept claims of power wrapped in the name of Christ, divisiveness, confusion and fear become pervasive in the church. For those who don't have a faith, without discernment they will be hard pressed to know what to believe. And even if the Christian perspective is inaccurate, deception is deception, and false claims of power must be exposed.

For me, believing in Christ is safe; following others who pervert what he stood for isn't. While there are those who have committed evil in the *name* of Christ, I have never witnessed someone who became evil by living as Christ lived and taught.

Exercising Faith

C. S. Lewis, one of my favorite authors, held the Chair of Medieval and Renaissance English Literature at Cambridge until his death in 1963. His shelf of writings is just as vibrant today as when his pen first met the page. He was never afraid to explore the depths of the Christian faith with intellectual integrity, (and it is his conventional approach with which I identify rather than the denominational route) and at the same time he never became so elevated in his intellectual pursuits that he couldn't express the same concepts in story form for young children.

In one scene in the BBC/Ken Curtis production *Shadowlands*—a poignant portrayal of Lewis's last years with his wife, Joy, whom he married late in life—is a thought-provoking question posed by his niece. Walking with Lewis along an English river bank, she asked how to accept by faith, no matter how well thought out, the totality of the incredible Christian story with all its obvious mysteries. Pointing to the river, Lewis remarked that one only learns how to swim by actually getting in the water. So it is with faith, he gently instructed. Dive in and learn by exercising faith, letting it become a part of you.

By "diving in," Lewis didn't mean that one neglects the mind and flirts with disaster. Before diving into a body of water, it's usually best to survey the scene. If it's winter you don't dive into a block of ice; and you don't dive into icy cold water without the proper gear and training. If the weather is suitable, checking out the depth of the water, location of rocks and the possibility of an undertow are all factors which require one to use the mind before taking the plunge.

I have seen people dive, without careful thought or scrutiny, into psychic encounters and other pursuits, quickly breaking their necks as they hit bottom. I have never seen someone take the plunge into the Christian faith as Christ taught and later regret it. There are those who will deceive using the guise of his teachings, but not the man from Nazareth.

So I close. I know that I have not answered all your questions. The subject of powers—real and counterfeit—is too vast to press together in one group of pages, but I hope that this has served as a good primer. Until the next time . . .

Notes

Chapter 2

[1]The station erased the videotapes before a copy could be provided to extract a word-for-word transcript, but the flow of the dialog is intact.

Chapter 3

[1]Thomas Saville and Herb Dewey, *Red Hot Cold Reading* (Denver: In Visible Print, 1984).

[2]C. R. Snyder and R. J. Shenkel, "The P. T. Barnum Effect," *Psychology Today,* March 1975, pp. 52-54.

[3]N. D. Sundberg, "The Acceptability of 'Fake' versus 'Bona Fide' Personality Test Interpretations," *Journal of Abnormal and Social Psychology,* No. 50, 1955, pp. 145-47.

[4]Ray Hyman, "The Psychic Reading," a paper delivered at the "Conference on the Clever Hands Phenomenon," New York Academy of Science. May 5-8, 1980.

[5]Ray Hyman, " 'Cold Reading': How to Convince Strangers that You Know All about Them," *The Zetetic,* Spring/Summer 1977, pp. 18-37.

[6]Ibid., p. 26.

[7]Donald T. Regan, *For the Record* (New York: Harcourt Brace Jovanovich, 1988), p. 74.

[8]*New York Times,* May 18, 1988, p. 13.

[9]John Townley, *Skeptical Inquirer* 11, No. 3 (Spring 1987), p. 265.

Chapter 4
[1]While I commend the practice of using quotation marks when referring to psychics in any news report, I have not considered it necessary to always do so in this book because my whole thesis questions the legitimacy of psychics.
[2]Keith Anderson, "Dallas' Psychic Detectives," *Dallas Morning News,* April 29, 1984.

Chapter 6
[1]The story, which had originated in Salt Lake City, had actually been on the wire for some time before the *Dallas Morning News* picked it up, and so Hydrick's appearance on "That's Incredible" had been on December 29, three days before I had seen the story.

Chapter 10
[1]Only a small portion of this interview was aired in the one-hour broadcast.
[2]This conflicts with his mother's statement that she left him when he was three *years* old.
[3]Hydrick's recollections of where, when, and with whom he lived do not always coincide with other reports.
[4]Astral projection is an alleged out-of-body experience in which one's spirit leaves the body and can return, all the while attached by a silver umbilical cord.

Chapter 12
[1]For a complete listing of every verse where these are referred to in Scripture, please consult a concordance.

Chapter 13
[1]This situation is not unique to ancient times. Today the study of quantum physics has taken on the same kind of mystical appeal. Simply stated, in quantum physics scientists seek to find out if there is one universal law over all other laws. For example, one might study to determine if there is a law over the law of gravity that influences it and/or allows it to work. A fascinating article appeared in the *New York Times Magazine* about the world's foremost authority on the subject—Dr. Stephen Hawking of Cambridge University in England. This is the reporter's introduction to the article:

> The theoretical physicist, although he deals in such arcane, modern concepts as curved time and space, is part of a philosophical and spiritual tradition older than recorded history. He seeks to know not just life as he experiences it but how the hidden parts of the universe work and fit together. Ultimately he hopes to learn if and how and why the universe

began and if and how and why it will end.

Dr. Hawking, a quadriplegic stricken with a progressive and incurable motor-neuron disease, shares some thoughts that convey the quasi-mystical pursuit in his studies.

The whole history of human thought has been to try to understand what the universe was like. . . . Even if God created the universe, we want to know what it is like. . . . One attitude would be that God set up the universe in a completely arbitrary way, with all that anyone can say about anything is that it is just the will of God. But in fact, the more we examine the universe, we find it is not arbitrary at all but obeys certain well-defined laws that operate in different areas. If we do discover a complete theory . . . it would be the ultimate triumph of human reason—for then we would know the mind of God. (*New York Times Book Review,* April 3, 1988)

Dr. Hawking's research is so far "out there" that for most us, we look on his intellectual prowess with an almost arm's-length reverential awe. Now imagine that a scientist like Dr. Hawking combined his theories and credibility with tricks like Hydrick presented, and that he attributed the source of his "powers" to his legitimate studies and theories of quantum physics. Many folks would accept his claims as fact because of his credibility.

It is in this same context that many of the *magos* moved and operated. They combined legitimate disciplines with pretended mystical pursuits. This helped to insure their political power and control over the common person, by appearing to have something more than just human knowledge—real supernatural powers.

²The Simon incident is very different from the one Paul encountered in Acts 16:16-18 where he cast out a demon of divination from a slave girl who kept hounding him in the marketplace. The woman was possessed by a spirit that enabled her to predict the future—which in turn was exploited by her owners to turn a hefty profit. If she was receiving "insider trading information" from an "undisclosed source," her business partners could use this successfully to increase their earnings. No wonder they were furious when Paul cast out the demon. This is the only example in the Scriptures where someone trying to predict the future apart from a revelation from God registered some success. I should point out, however, that to date I have not personally encountered such a case. That is, where it was clear that cold reading was not involved.

³In September of 1987 I attended a conference hosted by Scott Peck of religious and nonreligious professionals who had been involved with what they believed to be demonization. The informal consensus reached was the same as the Berkeley conference.

⁴From a personal interview.

Chapter 14
[1]Randel Helms, "Resurrection Fictions" *Free Inquiry* (Fall 1981), pp. 34-41.
[2]Ian Wilson, *Jesus, the Evidence* (San Francisco: Harper & Row, 1985).
[3]William D. Edwards, M.D.; Wesley J. Gabel, M.Div.; Floyd E. Hosmer, M.S.,
A.M.I., "On the Physical Death of Jesus Christ," *Journal of the American Medical Association* 225, No. 11 (March 21, 1986), pp. 1455-63.

Chapter 15
[1]Josh McDowell, "Campus Speaker Startles Students," *The Quest* (San Bernardino: Campus Crusade for Christ, 1983).
[2]Ibid.
[3]Josh McDowell, "Back from the Grave," an unpublished manuscript, 1987.

Chapter 16
[1]"I Sought the Lord," *The Pilgrim Hymnal,* 1904.

For information on obtaining video and 16 mm. films including

Psychic Confession
Kid Tricks

contact:
Korem Productions
P.O. Box 1587
Richardson, TX 75083